VERSIFIED ACCOUNTS

VERSIFIED ACCOUNTS

CLAYTON ALLSGOOD

ACKNOWLEDGEMENTS

I wholeheartedly thank my Creator, who blessed me with the talent and fortitude to get this momentous lyrical literature accomplished. I thank my parents for their words of encouragement, and my family for their love and support. The many performances, battles and freestyles I was a part of all were extremely beneficial for my development. To Kwasi Ramsey, thanks for your words of wisdom with regard to book publishing. Finally, a huge special thanks to Mia Redrick and her friendly, competent team. Mia made this complicated task of writing my first book as simple as possible. Mia was also paramount in making sure this book was developed efficiently.

This book is dedicated

to all lyricists who desire

to express themselves genuinely.

TABLE OF CONTENTS

FOREWORD

I was driven to write this book due to pressing circumstances. I had a lot of pent up viewpoints I wanted to lyrically showcase. My inner thoughts pushed me to be creative outside of conformity. I wanted to do something epic, authentic, and I was driven to make a new pathway which would allow my own words to shine alone on the strength of their own merit. I wanted to express myself differently using a different vehicle and outlet. I didn't use the conventional pathway of recording a musical rap CD. When marketing a rap CD, it comes with preconceived notions. The frequency of occurrence dealing with like elements, ideas, feelings and assertions, drugs, bitches, and money, with very little intelligence corresponding to the three.

For every action there is a reaction. This story by no means wishes to instruct one on how to walk the path of morality. However, like life, when paying attention, one can learn lessons. This book is for those who love to read fictional and/or nonfictional hood tales. Even though this story is fictional in nature, many of the things written here happen daily. This book is for those who want to read something serious, sexy and/or funny. Even for those who don't traditionally enjoy reading, they may find the elements of superior rhyme a surprising turn on. If you consider yourself to be hip-hop, or relate to any of the above reasons I just mentioned, this is a must read.

1
FATAL RELATIONS

It's a brisk, clear, beautiful fall day, in a suburb not far away, outside of Baltimore. Around 3:45pm, tranquility is interrupted by Melvin's shouts for sure. He clenches his fist, then punches his wife Rita in the mouth, it pours. Raged emotions, brains loco, and braids of hers he's choking her with. Neighbors hear commotion. Not in disbelief and risk intervening. Negative, only if there's an unusual need, damn.

Melvin steaming. Heavy breathing.

Melvin hollers out, "I found out about your scheming just now as I was peeing. Didn't know I was home early. Did I hear the convo, surely. You hop on the phone and talk stuff to another dude in my place. I hate Chauncey! Wait till I face him. I'mma waste him!"

She drops the plate when her face gets bashed in, and he backs her up. Jacks her up, slaps her up, cracks her up as she snaps her pumps. She clasps his thumb and bites it. She's in defense mode, yet frightened.

Melvin yells out, "You did it, admit it. You let him hit it. See my foot your tail is about to fit it."

She falls, but then punches him in the groin. Hits 'em with a pot. Boing! Melvin, angry as hell, makes his fist and her mouth join. She drops like a coin.

As their next-door neighbors' concern lessens, they envision all of the abusive noise in the kitchen.

Melvin yells out, "Rita, you're a squeezer. Cheater, you got me hot as fever!"

Rita murmurs, "I'm a deceiver 'cause you're an unloving, self-centered woman beater."

As she is trembling, time's pending, and she catches another one to the chin again, by the scuffed, blood-stained Timberlands. He smashes her optical lenses and said, "I knew it was him again. Your ex. He wants the Smith and West to red dot his chest flesh. I'm putting him and you to a rest."

Knock, Knock!

"Open up!" sounds one neighbor.

Melvin yells out, "Mind your business!"

Knock, Knock!

Rita yells, "Save me! Save me! Please, he's loco, crazy!" Rita's got more knots than rocks in Bedrock.

Caught in a headlock, gridlocked, Melvin says calmly, "This relationship is a dead flop. You went out of wedlock."

Bop, Bop! He makes her head pop.

She lays there as blood is gushing all on the floor. Melvin is deranged as he pushes open the door. As he runs to his Explorer, their neighbor, Ms. Bell, grabs her chest and yells, "Sure, sure! Run! The cops are going to get yah and God is going to fix yah!"

But the only thing Melvin can picture is making Chauncey's mom a griever and her only son blazed by the heater. Temperature's off the meter. He's ready to finish unloading as he's rollin' in the Explorer as if it was stolen. Holding his wedding band in his sweating hand, he knows he has exposed his instability behind the wheel. Now, hand on the steel, none chilled. For real, as wheels peel, he's hitting curbs and swerving, surging into emerging—traffic. Fifteen minutes later, he lets off the gas quick. Slams the brakes. Truck vibrates, shakes like quakes. His dead mates' mistakes are not justifiable. However acquirable, in retrospect, due to disrespect and how she was lied to. He killed his wife, now he feels he must take Chauncey's life, no matter how trife.

Hits the gas, runs the red light. Slim's crib is in dead sight. Hops out of the truck, wild and ready to start firing. Melvin's raged desire man—has Chauncey's future foretold. Melvin's feelings are sore and cold. He hits the doorbell. The door opens.

"Yo, why you gotta be an ass?" Chauncey asks. Chauncey, drunk and weeded up, continues, "Shit, I taught you was Rita's ass," and begins to laugh.

Melvin shouts, "She was my wife, motherfucker! I thought she had class." Melvin pulls out with a flash as Chauncey gasps.

Smack! Smack! Smack!

Melvin nails Chauncey all in his grill by the butt of his pistol, crazed in the mental. Before Chauncey can retaliate, *Bop! Bop! Bop!*

Two shots to his mug, see, right where his jug be. The third shot hits his groin. It isn't lovely. The whole scene is bloody ugly. For a full minute, Melvin doesn't budge. See, his future used to be promising, sincerely. But no longer. He's raged with pain and fury. Eyes red and teary. Vision bleary. His reality is too lonely and too scary.

Melvin utters, "Rita, I'm coming, here me."

Bop!

He goes the dead route. He puts his own head out.

Back in front of Melvin and Rita's house, their neighbor, Miss Bell, an old, skinny, frail 73-year-old woman, is shaking and crying. She's grabbing her chest, looking to the ceiling, asking "Why?" and -dials the phone. She kneels down close to Rita and whispers in her blood-splattered ear, "Rita, baby, you're not alone. Don't let your spirit roam. Baby, go home."

Just at that moment, the 911 operator asked, "How may I assist you?"

Miss Bell tries to pull herself together a little, even though she's emotionally brittle. With a disturbed voice, she says, "Oh my god, please get the police here right away, no delay. A woman was murdered, okay?"

The 911 operator responds, "What's the location?"

Miss Bell, shaking, with no hesitation, replies, "8108 Lakewood Drive is the cops; destination for this bloody, brutal situation. I knew this would come to fruition. Rita should have listened to my intuition."

The 911 operator continues, "Ma'am, where are you? Are you okay?"

Miss Bell asks, "What you say?"

The 911 operator poses the question again. "Ma'am, are you okay?"

Miss Bell, with a slightly calmer voice, says, "I'm fine. It's 8108 Lakewood Drive. Rita isn't alive. I wish… I… I wished she had survived. What a waste. What a waste."

As she sheds another tear trace that will grace Rita's face, she becomes overwhelmed by Melvin's damage of Rita and their place. Miss Bell mumbles to the operator, "I tried over and over again to tell Rita to leave, just please leave. Leave before that man rolls up his sleeve and chokes you until you can't breathe. Why don't you tell your father Steve? I met her mother a few…"

The operator cuts her off and said, "Ma'am, what exactly happened?"

Miss Bell responds, "Hmmm…. Well, I guess you think I'm flapping. Rita was shot in the head by her husband. Done asking?"

The 911 operator assures Miss Bell that the police are on their way. Miss Bell, justifiably still in dismay, says, "Okay." Then she turns to the doorway and with a demanding voice yells, "DJ! DJ!"

DJ is her nine-year-old great-grandson she's watching. She tells him to get his tail back in the house now. DJ's curiosity and excitement lead him to say, "Wow!"

Miss Bell yells, "Boy, do you hear what I say? Don't make me raise up and help you on your way! Now get, DJ!" Miss Bell turns her attention back to the operator and, with a stern voice, asks, "Where are the cops, darn?" That animal is long gone."

Miss Bell abruptly hangs up the phone, then stares at Rita in a somber zone and whispers to her, "Melvin will be punished," in an angry tone. She then leans in closer to Rita's bruised, bloody, lifeless body, crying with intermittent moans. Grabbing her chest again, shaking in her bones, she hears the sirens in the distance. Ms. Bell, still tense yet weakening, due to what she heard and the aftermath of this bloodbath, becomes more intense. She stares at Rita while most would be forced to turn away at a glimpse. Then the old, distraught woman states, "Men like Melvin are wimps. I could've shot 'im when he passed me. That would have been benevolence. Now I'm the one who has to call your mom and tell her this."

Under a spell of guilt, filled with could haves and should haves, the first officer enters. He looks at the old, little woman who appears to be devastated, and with a strong, determination in his voice, says, "Where's the douchebag? Did you see where he went? Ma'am, who committed this murder?"

Miss Bell, who has become suddenly disoriented, murmurs, "I heard yah. I heard yah. Ya'll must catch him before he goes any further."

After answering the same questions over and over again, Miss Bell sits on her steps. She ponders various steps and regrets. Maybe I should have told this person or that person. After about an hour of self-pity, Miss Bell gets an urge just then. "Oh my, I must call her." She dials her phone. Rita's mom answers the phone.

"Hello." Miss Bell, in obvious pain, says, "Paula, I'm sorry to call yah. This is awful. Ah… Melvin just murdered Rita."

Paula's heart feels weaker, and now the pain is deeper. She just lost her husband a couple of months ago, due to a massive heart attack. Miss Bell is unaware because neither Rita nor Paula told her that. Paula tells Miss Bell, "This cannot be true. Steve passed a couple of months ago and me and my daughters held it together like glue. Now this too. Rita's gone, my baby. I don't know what to do."

Paula cries loudly and breaks down completely. Miss Bell does too, feeling uneasy and needy. Needy to find out where is Melvin. Is he apprehended and soon to be a convicted felon? As Paula can still be heard crying, Miss Bell politely tells her, "I'm sorry," and hangs up.

She then turns all of her attention to the officers for answers to the where and what. Plus she also has a twisted feeling in her gut. That feeling of did someone else get snuffed could be stopped abrupt, only by an officer's response of no, not yup. In Miss Bell's eyes, Rita's tragic end is more than enough to endure. But she wants to be sure. She begins to explore the allure of numerous conversations between law enforcement outside of Rita's door.

It is now becoming increasingly dark, and only a few cops are left at the scene to drop in on as they talk. The first officer to arrive at the scene is Officer Riggs. He asks his partner, a rookie, "You got anything, kid?"

His partner says, "Not really. However, what do you know?"

Officer Riggs scratches his head and says, "Ok. Between witnesses and my radio, this domestic spat really was deadly, bro. A betrayal rage led him on this course. It would've been painful, yet more productive, to get a divorce. The victim's husband was Melvin Johnson. He owned a very large auto shop on the east side. Mrs. Rita Johnson's affair released Melvin's beast side. Lies and deceit, I'm sure each acquired. Far from benign, no denying, Melvin offed three people, including himself. Unstable emotional and mental health caused this love triangle to blow up like a stealth bomber. If Melv was calmer, he might have made a wiser decision, like split up. Instead of everybody being hit up. Left for dead, unable to get up."

Officer Riggs' partner, in a calm, yet unsure voice, suggests, "Maybe this guy Melvin was a wife beater and had a long history of violence."

For about ten seconds, there is silence. Then Officer Riggs loudly states, "Wife beaters are domestic tyrants! He should've walked away. In my book he's spineless. They made a bad choice. I've responded three separate times to this address for abusive disturbances and noise. Melvin had no poise. You know what; I'm not going to call you rookie anymore. Pete, you are going to be alright in the street. You got good instincts. Come closer, I need to be discrete. I heard Rita was a real freak on top of the sheet. She let quite a few guys beat, I mean beat. She had a beautiful head and gave beautiful head. A bangin' body and terrific in bed. Shit, you know what, I can see how Melv lost his head over that freaky fox he wed."

"You rotten, nasty bastard," Miss Bell says. Officer Riggs, in shame, drops his head and tells Pete, "Go on to the car, kid. Now Miss Bell, I'm sorry."

Miss Bell, angry as Hell, yells, "Yeah, you're sorry! Real sorry and ungodly. You know what bothers me, oddly? How you, as an officer, could stand in her yard and be making sexual jokes about a woman who had her life violently taken away today. Yeah, you are sorry. I heard what you been saying. Sir, this isn't the time or place to be playing. This is the site of a slaying. I was standing under the tree there, listening to your conversation, to be quaint. You should have locked up Melvin the last time and let an inmate take 'em out with a shank. I could care less if Rita wasn't a saint, to be frank. Ya'll, none of ya'll ain't. Now I'm going in my house before I faint."

Miss Bell's old, little frame hustles up to her front door and cuts her eyes at Officer Riggs before she slams it. Officer Riggs shakes his head. As he walks to his car, he mumbles, "Damn it."

GUYS HANGING OUT

It's 10:30 pm, and four guys are exiting a neighborhood bar they frequent. They started drinking hours earlier, no cheap shit. One of the guys named Richard says, "Yo, Ray, keep it. I'm not going to argue about some weak shit. My tolerance with you is depleted. Shut the hell up before I become heated! Pool isn't your game. Between all of us, I'm undefeated. Seriously, Ray, I don't want your 20 dollars. It's funny to all of us, keep it. Now take your drunk ass home to your wife, beat it. I hope she doesn't kick your ass. You reek wit' cigar smoke and tequilas, shit. By the way, that's too much to spend on a car that's two-seated."

Raymon fires back with, "At least I have a wife and I don't smell like *trees*, bitch." Then he hops into his brand new Porsche he's intrigued with. He adds, "I love my automobile, believe it."

Richard jokingly continues, "When your wife divorces you, you're going to need it."

11

As Ray pulls away, Richard hopes he'll make it home OK. Then he states, "The night is young, and I'm ready to play!" As his other two friends, not in dismay, laugh as Richard eyeballs down the few women that passed down there way like prey.

Richard is the one who stands out. Handsome, no doubt. Overconfident like a champ in a bout. He bops around with the presence of a lamp not out. In the midst of darkness, light he revamps—that's clout. 360 waves, sharp beard trim, fresh graze, various fades, ornaments, jewelry and apparel for days. What every woman craves and raves. He puts them in a daze by his smoother than the OJ's ways on stage. Within a material maze, a true ladies' man who pervades and persuades more dimes than appetizing entrées with caramel sundaes on trays.

He parades with straight As and no grays. "Let's blaze!"

Quinn says, as he exhales weed smoke from his face, "What's the place, and please don't drive fast. We're not in a race."

They all get in Richard's Jaguar XF. Richard's enthusiasm is on flex. He's ready to impress and mesh with females who are scantily dressed. Not to mention grab some ass and feel some breast.

The older and calmer one out of the three, Brother Wise, tells Richard, "We high and drunk, Rich. Shit, don't risk it. I know you don't need another ticket."

Rich says, "I got this, dog. We're going to Club Gifted. It's eight lights down, sharp right, don't let me miss it. It's ya'll first time here, I'm telling you. It's straight. Ya'll will revisit. It's exquisite, not to mention explicit."

Rich glances at the bottle in his console and pitches a fit quick. "Damn, you and Quinn damn near killed this fifth, kid. Pour what's left so I can get a sip. Shit!"

Wise asks, "Rich, whatcha mean explicit?"

Quinn comes in, "Please let his drunk ass focus in on driving. Dismiss it. "

Rich responds, "Hey, smart ass, kiss it!"

Raymon, Quinn, and Richard met in middle school. Now Quinn and Rich, as little fools, never let anything trivial chisel the two. However, Raymon, the other individual, felt invisible and at times, disregarded like tissue, too. Because even in the crew, he wasn't tight like glue. He wasn't outgoing as Rich and Quinn, who liked to fight too. Ray is small in stature and a little quiet too. He didn't brawl or ball. Neither did he have girlfriends to call. As they got older, he rarely drank and never smoked at all. Ray enjoyed watching Rich and Quinn get into stuff. Up until things were becoming increasingly rough and Quinn was rumored to be the one responsible for someone who got snuffed. During that time, Raymon started not to come around as much. He didn't stay that often in touch. He stayed in college. The street life of crime and possible time gave him no rush.

However, Quinn and Rich started hanging with Rich's older brother Lenard to get dollar signs. Lenard's main man then was Ryan, who now goes by Brother Wise. Between Lenard's connect and Brother Wise's knowledge and muscle, they began to rise into an enterprise. They crippled their adversaries to their demise. Lenard, Quinn, Rich, and Wise had their eyes on becoming multimillionaires. That was the guys' prize.

Brother Wise is five years older than Rich, Quinn, and Ray. He's done it all and can't believe he's here today. He's reluctantly celebrating his birthday, which was on Thursday. However, the crew thought Friday would make a better purge day. Brother Wise isn't as flashy as Quinn and Rich. He prefers to go unnoticed. Stay in the basement, read, and smoke shit. Tonight he agrees to redirect his focus.

Brother Wise used to be the wildest one out of the bunch. Quick to punch. Spit on your lunch. Blow out your guts. But after a lot of his friends got locked up and or touched, much of his demeanor changed to the contrary. When Lenard was killed a little over six years ago, his life of crime was over, surely. On his birthday weekend, Wise wants to converse with Rich shortly.

Wise is just waiting for the right place and right timing. He knows tonight isn't it, however he vows he won't stop trying to reach Rich before he catches one flying and his mother loses her mind and starts crying. The streets aren't kind, and he doesn't wanna witness another homeboy dying.

Fifteen minutes pass after their arrival. Quinn finishes off the remainder of the blunt, and the three are high as a kite too. Wise tells Rich, "Look, I know your mind is on who you're gonna lay the pipe to."

Rich cuts in, "Right, true."

Wise continues, "Rich, I would like you to call up Ray to see if he made it home safely. You know he seldom drinks, and it's late, G."

Rich says, "For heaven's sakes, G."

Quinn interrupts, "I'll hit him up before we go in this place, G."

The phone rings and rings. Quinn says, "Yo, he ain't answering. I hope nothing is a matter, man."

Rich, impatient, says "OK, let's go in and embrace this late night gathering. Ray is alright. Probably rattling from his Wife Tina battering and chattering. She got that man in check. Ray's drunk. That's it. Nothing to be tattling!"

Wise adds, "He's getting cussed out at my expense. It's my birthday, but to Tina that makes no sense. I feel a little guilty that his back is maybe against the fence."

Rich changes the topic with, "I'm tense, Melvin should be here, but he's with that wench."

Wise agrees with concern in his voice, "Rita. I don't like that bitch neither. When I go over to his house, I do my best not to see her. Melvin feels he needs her. His man card has been revoked. He's not himself. He's weaker."

Quinn jumps in, "I peeped her. Chauncey's been to third base more than Derek Jeter. I wanna smack the spit out of that whore, with my son's dirty ass sneaker."

They all commence in laughter and soon after make their way in the club for musical rapture.

Now Ray pulls in front of his house and staggers in. Tina immediately asks him, "Do you know what's happened to them?"

Ray's response is, "Huh, baby? What?"

Tina flags him in and says, "Come in here, the bedroom. I can't believe he capped them and -It's about Melvin."

As her eyes start welling, Ray's anxiety starts swelling.

She turns up the volume on the local news. Melvin's murders are the lead story from all the news crews. Tina asks Ray, "Did you know anything about their feuds?"

Ray replies, "Nope. Rich is still celebrating with his dudes, drinking booze. This is going to give them the blues. Mainly Rich. I wouldn't want to be in his shoes."

3
PLEASURE ESSENTIAL

It's 11:55 pm, and the club scene is popping. Quinn and Wise take in the scenery as Rich weighs his options. Quinn notes, "Yo, tonight this spot is rocking. I see where we can sit. Let's go up top, son."

Rich is pumped up and points out, "It's really crowded in this place, yo, but you gotta love the ratio. No time to waste, bro. The tiger's out the cage, yah know."

Rich is brash and out to have a blast as he focuses in on whose ass he's gonna smash. Quinn and Wise are really trashed as they both look for somewhere to sit cause they're out of gas. Rich leaves Wise and Quinn behind. He smoothly works his way through the packed crowd to grind and let his confidence shine. In his mind, *this night is mine!*

This atmosphere of so many women has Rich's radar tripping. It's so many for the picking. He feels like a boy in a toy store skipping. A sexy female brushes up against Rich and reacts.

"Wow, my girlfriends aren't fibbing or kidding. We were about to leave, but they saw you and told me what I might be missing. Now that I have a closer look, I wish I was in your grips and your lips are so good for licking and kissing. Please, don't get it twisted. It's not the martini that I'm sipping, but damn, you are so fine. I know you're in a commitment."

Rich responds, "Baby, not at all. You are a knock-out. Your tits look as if they're going to pop out. You look so good in that tight dress that's red. However, you would look even better in my bed. Not to get ahead, I'm surprised you haven't been wed. When you stepped in the door, over half these ladies should've fled."

She comes back with, "Please, come on. It's not enough for me to go around. But you look like you lie like a hound and get around."

Rich states, "Baby, everybody knows I'm bound to get around. Know this, I'm single and before the night is over, one of our bed boards is going to pound. Now how does that sound, you sexy brown…"

She cuts him off with, "I'm going to eat you like a mound."

As the DJ mixes in a dance hall instrumental, Rich continues, "It's so essential we exercise our potential. 'Cause this isn't coincidental, yet it's about to be coessential. Damn, lady, I'm so into you."

She confirms with, "It's hard for me to control my suspense too."

She then turns around and places Rich's grips on her hips and seductively utters from her lips, "You are hotter than sauce is. I want you to screw me where my loft is." She then rotates her hips with the precision of a dancer from Honolulu.

Rich says, softly in her ear, "I'm gonna do you. I love your accent. You're from the Caribbean. In bed, I'm smooth and rough like the environment of an amphibian. I'm the newly appointed honey dip recipient of the millennium. Yes, your curves, I'm feeling them. Work it, girl, put your hips on it. I got my grips on it. I see your gifts, flaunt it. Later on you can put your lips on it. You mad firm, no braw. I thought you had lifts on it. Shake it, shake it, shake it, but please don't break it. I want you to take it. Yeah, move it around like a swivel chair. Listen, dear, I'mma get you there and hit you there. No intermission here. I want inner friction here. Listen, dear, I rock expensive eyewear, yet best believe my vision's clear. My mission's here."

After 10 minutes of dancing sexually, she gazes into Rich's eyes and says effectually, "I want you sexually. Your place or mine? For thrills we could even do it in my Lex, you see."

Rich agrees, "I love the way you messed with me. I'm so glad you stepped to me. You keep on impressing me."

She replies, "I can see you undressing me and on top pressing me. You are truly one of a kind and so nasty. I know you're going to ask me. My name is Kathy. Now what's yours, before I suck you like taffy?"

Rich spins Kathy around and grabs her tightly from behind. He then kisses the side of her neck as he continues to grind. Just at that time, in a deep voice that's kind, "Miss, I'm Rich, and I'm going to scratch that itch as you wish."

Kathy feels his erection and responds, "Oh yes, with this. Mr. Rich, I saw you make your way to the dance floor. I moved in closer, hoping you would see me shake my phat ass more. You came to get your groove on. That's what you spent your cash fore. I rarely go out, but when I do, I got a knack for, fast forward, a straight dash for the crash bar. I know what to ask for."

Rich cuts in, "Your rack I wanna explore. The more I stare, my attention span collapses the more."

Kathy says, "You have all night to do more than just stare at them, for sure, Rich. Let me finish, when the bartender pours it. I'll tell him, I'll be back for more of it. Damn right, bring it on. Anybody thinks I won't go for seconds, better think on. I'm getting my drink on."

Rich's response is, "Bartender, one cosmopolitan and one Grand Marnier on the rocks. Kathy, you get mad props. I'm going to work you over like my Jag's shocks, or better yet, as if I was just released from Fort Knox. Yes, tonight I'm pulling no stops."

They both continue dancing, drinking, and singing. Kathy feels the tingling from Rich's fingers, and Rich gets an inkling, after this weekend, that they're going to continue to hook up for a couple more evenings. Kathy is ready to come out of her clothes quicker than water out of a faucet. She wants Rich to take her body, toss it, and sexually boss it.

Kathy grabs Rich and whispers in his ear, "I going to the restroom."

Rich's reply is, "I'll be waiting right here, miss."

Leaving Rich all up in the mix with a few guys and a whole lot of chicks. In Rich's mind, he feels he deserves this brand new sexual fix. Just at that moment, Brother Wise taps Rich's arm and notes, "You want to get your kicks messing with these chicks. Remember, when going raw, enter at your own risk. The bug is a terrible epidemic, according to the latest infection rate statistics. Everything I've said, dog, is realistic. Everything you do has good and bad consequences. So, Rich, use your head. The one with the senses. Don't be senseless and be caught out there all by your lonesome defenseless."

Quinn laughs and interjects, "Wise, you always be preaching. Rich, me and Wise are leaving. We're getting a ride with Nadia and Sheba, man."

Rich smiles conceitedly and says, "Yo, I'm the man. You can tell by the way I walk. 'Cause no matter how I talk, I'm pulling cuties with the fattest booties and it's all my fault. I got the combo to the vault. I hit 'em nice and wet. More than twice, I bet. After three times, like mice, I jet. I'm the type to pipe a shorty strong-arm style. But it's negotiable if the package is the bomb and wild. I peck it, wet it, get it, sex it, and exit. Yeah, I'm known to charm a spouse. Leave her exhausted with a torn blouse. Well, they're not for sale, but I've done porns on file. Banging ladies, I hope what they got for me continues to be wild. Every shorty I've worked over wore a smile. I can't help it yo, I'm a horny child."

Quinn laughs again and says lastly, "Whatever, Rich. Let's see if you remember the dame's name after tonight's flame. We know your aim. Me and Wise used to do the same. We out!"

As the music is pumping loud, Rich glances the crowd. He notices Kathy is talking to her girlfriends, looking in his direction with a total approval of their inspection. Rich, with a slight erection, strolls over to Kathy and her friends with a look in his face of hardcore sexing.

Once in front of them, he said, "Yes, sexy, I see you chilling with your girls, and I don't mean to pry. But this guy in your eye ain't too shy to give his pull a try. No bull, you're fly. My, oh my, only a fool would leave you high and dry. You know I'm not gaming. You would've been said I'm a lie and bye. You I'm eyeing, why? 'Cause we both want tonight spent with good excitement. Don't fight it. I'm the type, miss, to lay the pipe, miss, on the floor, the couch, and even the mattress. All facts, miss. I wanna smash this. I've had a lot of practice. I got the ride and so do you. No need for a cab, miss. If you come with me, you'll come again, due to my nastiness. It's no fronting in you. Now come on, put your ass on this."

Kathy looks at her colleagues as she blushes. "OK, I'm sorry to be rushing away. I'll see ya'll first thing, bustling Monday."

As Kathy and Rich are walking toward the exit to leave, Rich is feeling cooler than the outside breeze. Kathy takes Rich's sunglasses off and puts them on her face and states, "I hope you will fulfill my needs."

Rich's smooth response is, "I'll follow you to your loft, please. I saw you checking me out, and I know I'm the one you want to step with. Get real naughty, nasty, mess with, flex with, and have sex with. I know you'll catch my drift, like I know you'll catch my stiff. We can let our bodies mesh is the woods on the whips for kicks. I think we could and should. You look so good for flicks. I'm so perverted. I'm willing to work it and hurt it before I squirt it. However you like it. I can tongue you down while you slurp it and jerk it. I'm telling you, it's worth it. Let's burst it and become orgasmic. Unzip and hon grip--the sex addict. Let me at it. Let me stab it so good you'll call me Mr. Bang Fanatic. It's good when two people can come together on things, when they're at it."

Kathy concludes, "Baby, you are really on some mack shit. You know what, as you can tell, I'm stacked, Rich. Tonight, I'm going to let you have it."

Outside in the parking lot, they exchange phone numbers. It's a very cool night, but as a couple, they're hotter than mid-summer. As Rich follows Kathy to her place, his flesh hungers. Rich wants Kathy sexually, and Kathy wants Rich to take her to ecstasy.

It is a 25-minute drive. It's late; however, they are both awake and very much alive. Once inside of Kathy's home, Rich asks Kathy, "Do you live alone?"

Kathy's reply is, "Yes, I live alone in this big home. Now can you make me moan with your big bone?"

Rich casually says, "You know what, it never perplexed me intellectually. From the time you pleasurably, effortlessly brushed up next to me and got fresh with me perpetually. Indefinitely I would experience you sexually, unquestionably. Nextly or secondly, respectfully, it's a necessity. I admit your body is incredibly, unforgettably impeccable to me."

Rich holds Kathy firmly and continues, "I love our chemistry. Your symmetry sizzles me exquisitely. It's pinnacle to me, I make my entry into you physically, unequivocally."

Kathy says, "I love your intensity and suspense for me inquisitively. However, first we must give ourselves a shower. Simply a rinse, you see. Before you continue to kick it to me and give it to me eventually. Come, Rich, with me."

They take a hot shower and enjoy each others' bodies blissfully.

4

RICH GETS NEWS

It's 10:30am on Saturday. Rich has awakened to Kathy, who says, "I hope you'll like my eggs, pancakes, and syrup today.

Rich jokingly answers, "I know I like your legs, phat cakes and curves today."

Rich loves what occurred today. He says, "Thank you, baby, last night was a blast, right?"

Kathy confirms, "Yes, absolutely. You kept putting it on me, then you would shoot me acutely. You are such a cutie. Do you wanna spank my bootie?"

Rich looks around and asks, "Did you happen to see my cell phone?"

Kathy answers, "No, but I see your well-bone."

Then she positions per body to Rich's splendor. Rich then bends her, strokes it and enters her. After about 25 minutes of banging, they both are exhausted. Kathy afterwards says, "Your clothes, Rich, are in the closet."

Rich stands up and leans on Kathy's table. He thinks to himself, if he's capable, he wants her added to his stable. Kathy's a bombshell, far from a fable. He then leans over her, kisses her forehead and naval. Looks in her eyes that are hazel and says, "I don't know what else to say to you. Other than I want to see you again, not for a business appointment. I wanna see you again for your exquisite ointment. You have my number. Holler at me later and not for romance. You know, so we can have another heated, repeated performance. Baby, I love the workload you dropped on me. Girl, it was enormous."

Once breakfast is eaten and they were done, Rich gets dressed. He inspects and puts on his gun. The bedroom Kathy escorts him from. Both embrace the morning sun. Kathy looks at Rich and says, "I hope I'll hear from you soon, hon. I want us to have more fun."

Rich replies, "You will. We will. But for now, I have to run."

Rich quickly goes over to his car and hops into it. Turns the music up and starts rocking it. As he is driving, he notices his phone is in his coat pocket. He's glad he didn't lose it by dropping it. It is filled with messages. He listens to the last one left and thinks to himself, *Wise seemed vexed, yelling all in my phone, as if I'm deaf.*

He races home, 25 minutes away. To his dismay, two cops he knows personally are in the driveway. Rich gets out of his car and says, "Officer Powell and Morris."

Powell responds, "I know you're sore, Rich. I also know you don't talk to the law, Rich. Hey, I'm just a good cop who doesn't want to see you go to war for a bitch."

Rich, keeping his cool, but still baffled, says, "Officer, I don't dig, but you know what, do me a favor. Enlighten me. What the hell you talking about, pig?"

Powell smiles and says, "You really don't know shit. Uh, your boy Melvin is dead. He took out Rita and Chauncey, then put out his own head."

Rich pulls out a cigar and lights it. His anger has him ignited, but he doesn't want these cops to see him get excited. He knows they would be delighted, if he does anything to get indicted. He uses the cigar as a vice to fight it.

Officer Morris comes in the convo and says, "Rich, we didn't think it would go this far. We've been watching Grands and Chauncey from afar. We've also talked to Grands about what happened. He was just as shocked as you are. Nobody foresaw Melvin taking out Rita and Chauncey. Not to mention, Melvin leaving his own head ajar. You got anything to say, or are you just going to puff that cigar?"

Rich keeps puffing and doesn't say nothing. Officer Powell continues, "Grands isn't angry at you or your people, if that's any consolation. However, I just wanted to make sure there's no bad blood between him and you, if you know what I'm saying."

Rich's body language is still, but his energy is furious. He takes a few steps closer to Officer Powell and Morris and, in a voice that's serious, says, "What I'm about to do, you can't stop me. Now, both of ya'll, get the fuck off of my property."

Rich walks slowly into his house. Morris says from his mouth, "I hope he doesn't lose his top."

Powell adds, "I hope not, 'cause if he does, a few more are getting shot. It's been awhile since I had to use my glock."

After Rich takes a shower and changes his clothes, he listens to his messages and says to himself, "Everybody knows."

Rich then calls Quinn. He picks up and says, "Rich, hello."

Rich answers, "Dudes are shaky like Jell-o. I'm confronting Grands. He says anything slick, me letting it slide. Hell no! He's getting nailed, bro. I'll hit ya'll up later."

Click.

Rich leaves out and heads over across town. He's making his rounds. First stop is the auto shop he owns, which is called Melvin's. When Rich steps in, he sees Vince changing someone's belts and yells, "Yo, I need to holler at you, captain."

Vince stops. Rich says, "Yo, I know you heard what happened."

Vince says, "Yeah, Melv got tired of cats laughing. Cats were telling him Chauncey was also tapping. I told him to watch his back, man, because Chauncey was packing. I had a feeling somebody was going to get capped, man. Rita and Chauncey were seen all around town like a fire hydrant. Melvin left work early to surprise them. He fired them and expired them."

Rich is pissed off, then he yells, "Shit, I told him to leave her ass alone, damn! Look, Vince, you in charge, man. You been here as long as Melv and you know how the place needs to be ran. I'll talk to you about your pay increase later, understand?"

Vince then says, "Cool. When are you going to let the rest of the guys know, on Monday?"

Rich says. "Right, I'm going to sell you this place someday."

Vince adds, "Please, Rich, if you have an urge to do anything stupid, put the gun away."

As Rich walks to his car, he remarks, "Never that. I gotta run, OK?"

Rich hops in his Jaguar and peels out of the parking lot. His next stop is the salon he owns, and he's still hot. Rich's salon is just three miles down the street. Kathy texts him something sweet. However, Rich's focus is on picking up his money from the beauticians and giving Grands a surprise meet. Rich pulls up in front of his salon called Joyce's. His phone rings, and he answers.

Joyce's voice says, "Rich, I'm coming outside now. No need to get out. It's pointless."

Rich responds, "Do I have a choice in this?"

After about six minutes passes by, Joyce comes out of the salon, looking as usual, very fly. She switches over to Rich and says, "Hi."

She then walks around Rich's car and gets in. She counts the money out and gives it to him. Then she gives him a hug and states, "I'm sorry about what happened to him."

Rich strokes his waves and says, "Look, Melvin was the best worker. He was the backbone of that shop. I told Melv, Rita wasn't worth the…. Damn, I would be lying if I didn't admit this news wasn't a tear jerker."

Joyce reassures Rich with, "You know I am someone you can confide in. Your anger and hurt you can't hide and—that's why I didn't want you to come inside then. Rich, me and you go back. I always tell you how it is. It's just a fact. Routinely, Melvin was laying down the smack. Rita was a ho, but once it was out there like that, Melvin should have cut her off, crap."

Rich takes his sunglasses off and says, "I sincerely didn't know Melvin had these issues. This stupid act he committed was reprehensible. Everybody lose. When I first bought that auto shop from Mr. Williams, Melvin was there. Mr. Williams told me, 'Melvin was dependable, professional, and fair. Work was Melvin's only care'. A few times Melvin would come out with me and the guys, but not often. I put his name on the building 'cause, really, he was the boss man. The business was being run right. Melvin you could count on, so about us hanging out, I didn't hound him on. When he met that chick Rita, we all felt bad vibes in Melvin's demeanor. Melvin married her and made her a keeper. However, a good friend would've intervened and probed deeper. Alright, Joyce, how are you, Yvette, Nadia, and Sheba?"

Joyce holds Rich's hand and says, "We are all fine. Nadia and Sheba told me all of you had a good time. Don't beat yourself up over this. You are kind. This caught all of us by surprise, blind."

Rich hugs Joyce and says, "Tell Nadia and Sheba thanks for dropping my drunk friends off. Next week all of your rents are 50 percent off."

Joyce's response is, "Wow, oh my gosh! Thanks, boss."

Rich continues, "It's not like I'm taking a loss. Sometimes you need a friend to talk to before things can get resolved."

As Joyce gets out and switches across the street, she says, "Rich, you take care."

Rich pulls away slowly and says, "Yeah, I'll see ya'll later, dear."

5
GRANDS AND WISE TALK

Grands could make a hustler who's materially overzealous jealous. The king of story tellers. Loves to relish--in telling a story that's been embellished--about urban dwellers, gorillas, and killers, in an environment that's hellish, quicker than propellers or rain that brings forth fella's umbrellas.

As Rich searches around town for Grands at places he may be, Grands pulls up in his Audi A8 in glee. He catches Wise hanging like drapes be, in front of his barber shop as he always does during this time faithfully. He yells, "It would be gracious to me if you would get in and have a face to face with me."

Wise is reading a newspaper at the time, waiting on a client patiently. He wants to talk, but doesn't want to come off hasty. Wise folds his newspaper up, gets into Grands' ride, and says, "What brings you to my place, G?"

Grands goes on to say, "You know how the rat race be. I'm on a paper chase, you see, from state to state, G. Lately I haven't had to put a hole in anybody who's shaky like a pastry in a bakery. Snakes be wanting to graze me, blaze me, waste me or erase me. The streets never amaze me. I've been telling Chauncey for days and days, see, to leave Rita alone gracefully. Give her the brakes, please. Now my man will be missed greatly. A woman doesn't make me. I got women who wait for me to squeeze them in on my schedule to date me. No headaches, please. Whatcha wanna say to me? I'm conceited, yeah, that's your take on me. Fuck it. My clothes are strictly spiffy. My automobiles are nifty. I keep a glass of Henney or whiskey. I got dimes that are switchy from Tiffany to Misty, for me to knock out the park like Ken Griffey, whenever I wish, G. A trigger finger that's itchy and please, figure I won't miss, G. Money stays with me. I'm Grands. Grands in my hands stays sticky. I'm so gritty and witty in any damn city. You'll never catch me slipping, even when it's slippery. You can believe it or not, like Ripley. For any committee who wanna come get me or hit me will feel shitty. Fuck the bickery and or trickery. The hollow tips will give 'em an epiphany, vividly, swiftly. I'll make 'em history. The jurors will acquit me. Yeah, give me the victory. My lifestyle so iffy and risky. It's all or nothing with me. My product stays on the move like a gypsy. It's street wizardry. Life's really bitchy. I stay on the grizzly until I'm put in a ditch, see, what's up with your man Richey? It's a pity, a real cat died over a bitch, agree?"

Wise's response is, "Regardless of how you feel about Melv, they're goners, G. It bothers me 'cause what they did was strongly wrongly, honestly."

Grands agrees and continues, "I know. Let me share a story with you, bro, before you go. Yo, catch the verbal illustration. This is an ill situation of a cat so chill, his demeanor is cooler than refrigeration. He puts shorties out like liquidation. Fuck the insinuation. No guessing. His profession is the boss of ho rental sessions. His alias I can't reveal. He packed steel and wheeled a lime green STS. He rocked a large ice piece which inscribed I'm blessed. The medallion took up half his chest. Test the kid. Yes, he'll flex a sly smirk, pull out a knot of hundreds from the gold money clip. Then pull your honey dip after his bodyguard introduces you to the dummy whip. That's slang for putting size 15 in your tail. He rocks a greasy, phony tail. What he gots for sale, keeps his pockets swell. Hell, he doesn't walk. He strolls. What he holds is chicks who dress scantily and or trampee. Plus, their income, and then some. Despite the flashy, clashy clothes and demeanor, he's not exempt from some public ridicule. Shit, he's a pimp. He rocks loud, colorful custom made suits. Gaiters to match. A fur coat to match the fur hat. He often calls his employees Bs when he doesn't know where they're at. Lenses slightly tinted. He would admit he's a 70's flash-back. He loves the girls who grew up on the fast track. Bring 'em in, he'll polish their act. Best chick was a girl named Harmony. She told him calm-ly, 'Daddy, I got you a new freak who's phat. I'm telling you, baby, she'll increase your stack.' The pimp said, 'Yes, I need to meet her' and when he did, he said, 'Baby got back, a nice big bubble, and a huge rack. I'm blessed like my medallion says on my chest. Let's get you working. You make me feel like jerking. First I need to know if you know how to work it for cer-tain. Now it's time for you to take a ride on my pole, B!' The pimp rocked her daily, like his gold teeth, goatee, and brand new Rolle. After about two weeks of working, the pimp said, 'Pinkie, hold me. Somebody told me—you wanna leave me. What's the problem? You good? My money is cheesy. We're a good team. I need you, you need me. The clientele is needy, and the money is speedy. Why you wanna impede me, you read me? I don't want you to leave me. I want you for keeps, B.' Pinkie replied as she cried, 'My father knows what I do and about you. Hell, he knows you.' The pimp was like, 'So, who cares, boo. Even if that's true.' Pinkie then hollered out the pimp's real name. The pimp looks confused and thinks, *What's wrong with this crazy, drugged-out dame?* Pinkie screamed, 'I'm your niece! My father, your brother, wants me to go home, and he's putting two in your dome piece.' Now the big shot pimp is feeling lower than a maggot, to say the least. He had sexual relations and prostituted his own niece. Pinkie went on to say, 'When I talked to my father on the phone and gave him your name and location, my father told me you are my uncle and I started shaking. Since he has told me this, all I've been doing is crying, pacing and aching.' Pinkie's ex-pimp mumbled, 'No, no, nah, it can't be, as he walked away with a limp. Life stood up and backhanded the pimp."

Wise asks, "Alright, dog, what's the moral of this tale? Please tell."

Grands points out, "Yo, people who's close to you—do the most to you. Sometimes physical, sometimes emotional. Usually it's both, too. It's important to watch your greed. It's also just as important to watch your deeds."

Wise scratches his head and says, "Come on, man, I learned that shit decades ago. Nevertheless, I got something I need to say to you, bro. First of all, it's not about me dissing you. I just want you to listen to—what I'm trying to get across. We all take a loss until we decide to be responsible, as well as the boss. I know about some of the shit you got. Fifty grand watch, knots, yachts, and mad stocks. Player, you're top notch—in your field. I can tell by the rocks you flex on the real. You make a brother yield—to steal a closer look at your wardrobe. Chicks who surround you scheme to be the one walking around in your robe after getting you off for the night. She may not seem bright, but she's plotting on your dividends. You know it, 'cause your game is tight. You got a bachelor's degree in player's education. Playetts only like rich players to play with when funds are decaying. I know my personal opinion is weighing. Remember what you're doing. I already did. Know what I'm saying?"

Grands is annoyed. He fires back with, "People like yourself can be a bug to me. I got numerous chicks pampered in luxury. They're on my tip, very little fuss to me. Wise, they better enjoy it while they can get it because with the swiftness, I'll give the stiffness to the next girl who's uncommitted. In a player's mind, untapped prospects is forbidden. I ain't kidding. When I pull up in front of a chick's apartment, I got condoms assorted in my glove compartment. Chicks be half dressed, obsessed outside, bringing on my enlargement, before I can pull the GS in a space to park it. I live it. I just don't talk it. I walk it. Any asshole tries me can catch my hawk spit and the end of my 45 target. I'll stretch his ass out like carpet. I'm sharp with it, smart with it, and it's an art. I'm demented. The streets is the sea, and I'm the baddest shark in it. I got the heart to win it. As for the chicks, yeah, they just wanna manipulate you. I tell them to their face, I just wanna penetrate you. Since my cash is the only thing that really stimulates you. The upshot of my enemies who plot will be found fatally shot. I'll tell yah, I got stocks, yachts, and knots. The hell with the courts and the cops. You talking about Jessup or Hagerstown. Please, I'm a rich hustler, slash player now. No way I'm checking in corrections for inspections. I stay flexing. Intimidate who, incriminate who? Snitches, please, I got the bread to make heads ask, eliminate who? Hell, I got a bomb specialist on my payroll who could disintegrate you. I'm all about the bread. Fuck who bled or who winds up dead. My team is the one to dread. Enough said."

Wise, in return, presses the issue. "OK, for the sake of argument, you got more hons than a bakery has buns. Plus large sums of cash to flash like rich diplomats' sons. Whips so fat it stuns the average Tom, Rick, and Nick. Chicks you bang from all corners of the earth, yet your worth doesn't look favorably on your own turf. You see, you rather drop greed instead of seeds. That's, in part, why so many of us bleed. Indeed, you got mad expensive things. You got things to keep the chicks staring. You got things to keep the crooks staring. You got things to keep the Feds staring. You got things to keep them all staring, hearing, and preparing. Things to keep you self-centered as you be flashing it. Things in which how you bought it, will have you in a cell, saying damn it. You have things which will have you missing as your people panic. The only reason why you're able to hustle is because you're the man at it. In addition, some gangsters in the government planned it. To speak candid, the truth isn't outlandish. My soul demands it. Me and Lenard ran shit. We expanded on cats who were underhanded. Weight we transit with the precision of a praying mantis. Avoided wire taps and cameras. Yes, they couldn't handle us. Geniuses, I guess, among addicts, yes, and weight handlers. It was our planet impressed. Competition got frantic and vexed. They got banished or managed to vanish like a Manwich sandwich. We had the advantage. Far from average, nonetheless, for the hood, we did mammoth damage. Understand this, we need to get on some self reprimand shit. I'm building two community centers. How about you lending a helping hand in this? I could use your help to finance this."

Grands hesitates, then answers, "Listen, if you exercise the plans, son, I mean man, handle them. Fuck a memorandum. One of my dogs will make a standard run from the mansion at random. Yeah, to hit you off with Grands' son for the expansion."

Wise agrees, "Right under the radar like a phantom. I'm excited as a kid in camp or something. When we rebuild, we're hood champions with accolades thrusting."

They both give each other dap, and neither man is bluffing. Wise gets out, feeling more than a tad glad on what they had in a rush discussion.

Wise begins to step away from Grands' Audi. Grands rolls the window down and yells, "Yo Wise, my memory is cloudy! One more thing before I'm out G."

Wise walks back over, then leans in his passenger window with his head and shoulder. Grands puffs a huge blunt, then says, "Dog, I gotta be up front. What Rich boy did Melvin, it really stunk like a skunk. He played himself like a straight punk. Killing everybody over some unloyal pussy. He was a chump! That wasn't a good reason to make his pistol dump. Now listen, I'm not going to start and end some junk. But yo, for a minute I thought my major boat might have sunk!"

Wise shakes his head, having an idea what Grands is referring to. Grands' next statement will confirm it is true. "You know Chauncey was my right hand man. Me, him and Rita had a plan to take over most of this city, understand. Nobody would be able to compete with our brand. But oh no! You know what happened next my man. Melvin goes blam! blam! I was mad vexed, know what I'm saying. There goes my partner and our connect. Out of effect. I was a wreck. Between the personal and financial loss, I was like what the heck, for a sec. Then out of nowhere, I get another super cool connect. This person I'm about to meet. Whom I haven't yet met. A similar sweet deal is on the table. It's a bet! Now I'm no longer upset. Ain't that some fucking crazy shit. Another thing: when Melv decided to dead them and make the rounds of his .357 embed them; my new connect said at that moment she had to take two Excedrin."

Wise shakes Grands' hand and says, "Looks like your loss now is only personal. Make sure I'm informed about the funeral. I know that in itself still hurts you."

Wise somewhat quickly walks into his shop as if he has a curfew. He doesn't want to hear Grands, who is still a little pissed, say something about Melvin more hurtful.

Wise, disgusted, mumbles to himself, "Melv, if you were alive, I would curse you. Then my fists would make your lips burst, fool. Long before Grands' people had a chance to Earth you."

Wise sits in one of his barber chairs, sees his reflection in the mirror and thinks as he stares, *I know we were never that close, and now you're ghost. You was a good dude, but, dog, you fucked up to the utmost.*

INDIGNATION
(LET'S DO IT)

It's now 20 minutes past four. Rich's feelings and maybe dealings with Grands have him sore to his core and ready for war. However, he wants to know for sure before he utilizes the option of putting Grands on the floor.

I'm not the one to ignore, Rich thinks to himself as he is driving. Rich is cool with Grands, but at times, he knows Grands can be conniving. A meeting he's desiring, so Rich can feel how he's vibing. Did Grands pass his message to Chauncey, or is he just jiving and lying? Rich's assignment is to get his point across like a trident. No denying it. He's frustrated as an innocent man in confinement. He's obsessed and seems to be losing his mind quick. Rich's face is twisted with anger, no disguising it.

As he searches various establishments for Grands' whereabouts, he gets the sudden inclination to stop by Grands' warehouse. He's sure he's there, no doubt. He wants the confrontation now, so he can air it out. As he accelerates his Jag, it's the only thing he cares about.

In front of the warehouse, there's five guys who are in deep conversation to no consternation, about who's facing exoneration and stars they would like a closer look at. Not the ones part of a constellation. The ones that come with an accommodation and maybe provocation.

They individually verbally fantasize a variation within a vacation of sexual exploitation and rival thugs' evacuation during times of inflammation. Dialogue also surrounds the verity of a certain colleague's accusation within the association which threatens the foundation. On this particular occasion, they also just got finished chowing down on take-out that's Cajun.

As the work crew pulls off from finishing the last stage of renovation at the obscure, remote industrial location, Rich, filled with anger in heavy rotation, no invocation, pulls up on the five guys, jumps out and states, "Here's a verbal illustration. My 45 will go blazing and do some heavy penetration if I don't get some information! Who wanna demonstration, 'cause I'm feeling nothing but frustration! By the way, I feel no intimidation. I'm not an imitation. Fuck your insinuation or maybe your bitch insemination. I'm Rich. That's my identification. Fuck an invitation to your congregation or maybe even your celebration. I'll burn a hole in you, you, you, you, and take out the other with asphyxiation. From the look on your faces, this wasn't this evening's anticipation."

The taller one out of the five, named Clyde, says, "Goddamn, you better beat it before I become more heated. I'll bust my 40 cal. And make you eat it, then excrete it. I'll separate your spirit from your physical. Yeah, free it. The ground we stand on, I'll put you beneath it. Matter of fact, I think I wanna see it. Your life will be depleted, deleted, obsoleted, you'll be unable to repeat it. I'm undefeated. Motherfucker, at minimum you'll become a quadriplegic. You and your God, believe it."

Rich readjusts one of his rings and cracked his knuckles, then says, "You gonna do something, you mad? I'll knock you out and choke you out with your do-rag, you fag. Fuck, I got a problem with your boss. Tell me where he's at, or take a lost."

Clyde, with a mean, yet careful look, says, "Rich, the problem you got yourself into is tremendous. You can't win this since Grands is so disingenuous, then end this. He'll have your ass on the run like track stars in the Olympics. Spinning rounds will hit your appendix and cause you to spin around like a gymnast. Your street rep finished, unable to be replenished. Hell, Rich, you frail bitch, how you gonna come up in here, play judge, and give us orders like we bailiffs?"

Rich laughs and jokingly says, "Well, bitch, you all are under surveillance. You know what that translates to? Ya'll ain't about to kill shit!"

One of the five dudes named Rodney, who's stocky, forcefully says, "Get the fuck off of our property."

Rich smirks and asks, "Or what? You're going to clobber me? Please, if I wanted, I could take Grands' monopoly. As for you, step off before you get dropped properly."

Rodney steps to Rich, and his response is, "Yo, I'm confused, Rich. Now you're really playing yourself like cue sticks or acoustics. Mr. Loose Lips, you're working with the law now. Damn! You got any more exclusives."

Rich calmly answers, "Dog, you should know I'm really intrusive."

Quickly Rich spits in Rodney's face and whips out his 45 and smacks dude's lips. Then he shouts, "Ahh haa! Look at who drips. You frail like tulips." Rich, pointing his 45 at all of them, adds, "I'm unamused, chicks. No, I'm not working with the cops!"

Rich then punches Rodney in his bloody mouth and kicked him in the crotch. Rodney crouches and continues to the ground as Rich, with a demented frown, relentlessly continues to stomp and pound and pound and pound until Rodney doesn't make a sound. Rich then proclaims, "I wish one of you motherfuckers would make me squeeze off a round!"

Rich, pointing his 45 at all of them, yells, "I don't know if ya'll are under surveillance or not. I lied to keep you all from grabbing a glock. I do know if ya'll don't cooperate, all five of you assholes is getting shot! With the exception of the dude who's sleeping on the ground, kids. The four of you put your hands on your heads."

The four of them do as ordered. One of the four, named Dana, mumbles, "I wish my Ruger wasn't in the Land Cruiser. I would shoot yah."

Rich lashes out at him, "Right now my heart is colder than winter in Vancouver! It would behoove yah to watch what comes out of your mouth before I shoot yah. Loser, I'll execute yah!" Rich then abruptly shot out the rear window and two tires on the Land Cruiser. Then he shouted, "From the time I pulled up on you clowns, I had you all measured up like a ruler! I know Grands and many of the top dogs in ya'll organization. Yo, fuck ya'll cats faking, perpetrating, and hating. This here is the situation. None of you clowns got any type of rank. Trust me, this isn't no type of prank. If you lie to me, that's your life. You all can take that to the bank. Don't make me pop the trunk and pull out the tank."

As one of the five lay unconscious, the remaining four look at each other, thinking to themselves. *I rather be in the slammer than this. The grammar of Rich is beyond the glamour and glitz. This pretty motherfucker gots a 45 in my face, handling this.* None of them want to get hit by the hammer of Rich.

Rich, pacing back and forth, mugging, goes on to say, "Yo, I feel like a guy who didn't get his pension. I really need to talk to Grands, so I figure this will get his attention." Rich then bangs Dana in his face with the 45, presses it on his eyelid and continues, "You dumb fuck, do you see where I'm coming from now? Shit, listen, your lid is dripping. Tell me where your boss is at before I commit a rendition on your man and give him a permanent affliction. Yeah, worsen his condition. I'll be the reason for his benediction. I ain't kiddin'!"

Another guy named Dan pleads, "Come on, man. Please be a little sensitive. We are all on the defensive. I'll take the initiative. I don't want to get put in care that's intensive. We don't know where Grands is at. That's that…it's repetitive."

Rich commands, "Then tell me how can I reach him, unless you want a permanent sedative! That goes for not only you and them, but a relative…yeah, it's relative."

As Rich continues to point the 45 at Dana's head, another guy, Curt, speaks up and says, "How can you let Rita and Melvin, sir, stress you're your vertex? Ask around about Rita if you're perplexed. My first guess, you must want to join Melvin on purpose… That whore's sex was powerful as a vortex, and she was for raw sex. You never knew who was creeping out of that whore's door next. Rich, our man Chauncey died, too. The 357 was the last thing he saw flex. To make this plain, we all have much pain to sustain. Neither you nor Grands is to blame. I don't know your aim, not to mention, why you came. Rich, don't fuck with Grands' reign. Chauncey got banged to his brain. Shit, we all are hurt, know what I'm saying?"

Rich screams, "Asshole, I don't care about your hurt or possible priors, man, sirens, man, whether or not if you're on the wire, man, or whose hiding, possibly eyeing, spying this time, man! Fuck this empire. Damn! In my prime, man, my money was wider, man, when I was thriving. You're lucky to be alive, man, because normally when my bullets get the flying, everybody's dying. Especially when I don't get what I'm desiring and or requiring. I should be splitting a dime Hawaiian hymen instead of frying and perspiring—to the point where I'm the reason ya'll motherfuckers are expiring."

Curt comes again, "Grands got plenty of muscle with an extended clip for guys like you with extended lip. Fuck it, you can kill us, but you and your men will drip. On the real, he could dispose yah if he chose tah. Simply put, soldier, you and your peeps' emotional rolla coaster will be over."

Rich snaps, "I'm deadly as a cobra when I bang more shots than Villanova. I can show yah. My 45 is out the holster, and I'll nail you all to the wall like a poster. I'm not a jokester or imposer. Fuck our lives. This loud-mouth vulgar boaster will kill you all quicker than a Long Island I sit on my coaster." Rich then quickly shoots the emblem off the truck, which is Toyota.

Then he continues, "Yeah, I'm the epitome of grimey B'more. Problems, it'll be more if you get in my way, you'll know you should've hit a detour. I'm far from meager. I'm eager to bust shots at leisure. I transported more keys, whore, across the seashore. Life's ups and downs, like a seesaw, has me hot as a fever or cold as a freezer. I wheeze more, yet I smoke trees more. B'more we war. I'm deadly as a seizure. I still get G's whore, could care less how you feel neither. I play for keeps, whore. Now the predicament you all are in is terrible. I'm irritable. Other than the Henney and weed, you know what sooths my nerves, too. Trashing motherfuckers like items that's perishable."

Rich reaches in his car and pulls out a beer. He takes a swig and states, sarcastically, "Be a dear. Tell Grands I was here." He then gets in his Jag and has a silly notion. He turns up loudly Billy Ocean. He pulls away as Dan, Dana, Curt, and Clyde stare, pissed off, yet frozen. Rodney finally picks himself up off the ground and says, "Rich is toast, son."

Rich zooms out of the proximity, thinking to himself, *Those cats are shrimps to me, chimps to me, wimps to me. That one dude was stocky but flimsy to me.* Rich then pulls out his cell to hit Quinn. He's going to let him know what just went down with an evil grin.

When Quinn answers the phone, he abruptly says, "Right now I'm playing with my son, then I'm going to get in a quick nap, man. Hurry up. What happened? Start jibba jabbing about your antics and I know I'm going to need an aspirin from my cabin again."

Versified Accounts

Rich commences to go off, "At times the streets make me wanna simply flip. Make me wanna empty a clip. Leave cats' physical frame empty and drip. Life's simply a bitch. The world is yours. I take what I can. We're headed for simply a ditch. Nobody's exempt from this. No one should be stepping to me. I'm stressed and ready to be pressing an uzi. I'm trying not to let me sanity lose me. I try to keep a cain mental, but sometimes I want a motherfucker to feel pain from my pistol. I want a motherfucker to die. I'll kill an asshole and his alibi. I didn't tell a lie. I know it's going to happen. My gun's clapping – bet. It's like the world's a big entrapment. Fools want me to blast shit. Want me to splash shit. Want me to put 'em in a casket. It's like I need to rack the slide back and catch a homicide rap. Murder the fucking snitch who looks like he's ready to drop a dime back. Smack a fool, then ask what the fuck is he eyeing at. These young fools don't know me, fucking phonies. I see the bitch in half of those fools clearer than a 60 inch flat screen Sony. In fact, it's one son of a bitch I wanna kill, in particular. If we cross paths, I'mma show him I'm more sicker when I squeeze the trigger. I'll bang up everybody in his house. His seeds, his spouse, anybody with mouth. Spit on his baby picture before exiting the house. Burn the bitch down, kill everybody. Yeah, the roaches, the mouse. It goes for everybody towards me who wanted to put a spark out. My goal's to put their fucking heart out. I'll have cats in suits who put chalk out. Leave my shell cases with no prints, purposely for them to talk about. Fuck it, death's inevitable. My rage is incredible. I'll put the gauge in an asshole's mouth as if it was edible. Blast his skull fragments all over his living room. Turn his living room into his dying room. That's what I call using his brains, unforgettable!"

Rich then forces a demented laugh and tells Quinn exactly what he just did. Quinn, not completely annoyed, scratches his head and says, "You are going to take this as being cynical. What you did, at minimal, is insensible, and you're too damn visible. You carried shit as if you're still in the game and invincible. Shit, I knew it. You had to lose it and do something incredibly stupid -before I could convince you to cool it. Whatcha got to prove, Rich? My son is calling me. Until later, hold yourself together like glue, shit. Rich you know what!" he pauses, then tells his son to "hold up!"

45

Quinn shakes his head, then continues, "I know you see red, but are you trying to wind up dead? All of our teams who is still out there in the streets not doing time, confined. Now work for Grands, have you lost your damn mind! Rich, you me and Wise are not moving weight anymore. Get it straight, me and Wise feel great, galore. Personally I'm not looking to go back through that door. Looking for a big score. I got a wife and son to care for! We are legal businessmen. You want to act stupid now! Yo, this must end. When Wise isn't boxing he's mentoring kids at the gym. None of our pockets are slim. Neither is our condition grim. Your actions today is sicker than phlegm. Between all three of us, we own about two million in properties. Your brain needs a tune-up like the autos at your parking lot shop, Jeez. Me and Wise gotta smooth this shit out before your top gets popped with ease. I know when you rolled up on those cats, they were in shock Jeez. You need to chill out and put your mouth on lock please."

When Quinn hangs up, Rich seems to calm down at last. Suddenly, just at that moment, Rich notices an unmarked cop car rolling up on him fast, as red and blue lights in its grill flash. Rich quickly pulls his Jag over on the side of the road. He notices Powell and Morris running over towards him as if they're going to explode.

Powell loudly orders, "Get the fuck out of the car! Your stubborn, hard-headed ass went too far!"

Rich calmly gets out and, in a relaxed demeanor, says, "Guys, chill. Nobody's guts got spilled or killed."

Morris gets in Rich's face and says, "You really must want it." Then he gives him a sharp, hard punch to his stomach. Rich isn't about to do some dumb shit like knock Morris out or go for the gun quick.

Powell instigates, "Come on, Rich. You're going to let him pound your ass?"

Rich, pissed off, yet calm, states, "Right now I'm going to respect his badge. Look, I'm not trying to fuck up ya'll investigation or test ya'll patience. I'm not dealing with Grands anymore or anybody in his operation. Powell, you have my full cooperation."

Rich readjusted his tinted lenses, then, asked, "What's up with the inflated tempers, men? You a friend of them? I just shot out a couple of tires and—a window, men, at minimum just to be offending them. Oh, not to mention, men, also an emblem, then let my tires spin on them. Only after I spit phlegm on him, I checked that simpleton's chin again and again. I thought he was going to wet his denims then, as his blood was dripping then. I had to knock him off his equilibrium and leave him trembling like a wet gremlin, for boosting my adrenaline. I had a conniption then. Hey, I could've been more deadly than venom and—made it grim for them. I could've took two 45s as I was gripping them, individually pop ten in them 'cause I got plenty of clips for them. However, I didn't, men. Nope, I practice discipline, so see, I really wasn't tripping, men. Grands isn't my nemesis, men, however, those clowns in regard to his reputation are a blemish on him." Rich smiles and sits back inside of his Jaguar. Once inside, he reaches for a cigar.

Morris, puzzled, says, "Powell, let's take him in. We're the law."

Powell ignores Morris as if his comment is of no concern. He then walks over to Rich, grabs his shoulder firm. Then, in a voice that's stern, "One way or another you're going to learn. Oh yeah, motherfucker, you're going to learn. The only reason you're not in bracelets is because your brother Len intervened and kept my father from being wasted. Oh yeah, you wanna hang that over my head. I can see that. I don't need a recap. That fucking robber shot out my old man's kneecap. Lenard happened to be there, and he killed him before it went any further. He kept my father from being murdered. My father retired and got his pension. Yeah, and in return, I turned the other way when your people was having that dirty money rinsed, then. That was then, this is now. No more favors, pal. If I see you anywhere near Grands, I'm putting you away for a very, very, very long while."

Rich blows smoke in Powell's face and says, "Alright, I'll stay out of sight."

Powell adds lastly, "I'm going to pretend what you made occur is now a blur. Now get the fuck out of here, as you were!"

Rich agrees, "Sir, I won't defer. I absolutely concur." Then he pulls off into what was the evening, but is now the night.

Now Morris turns to Powell, more than uptight. Ready to ignite. "How could you let that asshole take flight? With all of my might, I'm trying to avoid a fight! I'm telling you, your boy ain't that bright! He gets in the way, it will be my delight—to make sure his head gets blown away like a kite!"

1

CONVERSATION
FOR THOUGHT

Right now it's a little past 6:30. Quinn and his son Kyle are hungry, dirty, and thirsty. They race each other towards their house to see who'll be first.

"See, this is what I'm talking about, guys. Don't track dirt on my floor. Open your eyes," Quinn's wife Patrice says. Then she pops Kyle with a dish towel across his thighs. "Boy, don't look at me surprised that I have a rise. Ya'll need to wash yourselves up. I made two sweet potato pies."

Before Kyle goes upstairs, Quinn hugs him and says, "Son, I have something I want to share."

Kyle says, "Dad, yeah."

"Little man, don't be embarrassed when it's your turn to pitch. I must assert this. I urge this. You need to learn this. I give you words to nourish and encourage your merits so that you flourish. Yes, your knowledge and courage. You, I cherish. Your mother would concur this. I love you and your mother in marriage. I gave her major carats before you needed a carriage. Anybody like a stern itch tries to inflict harm to us like a terrorist, could expect to be burst with – and immersed with – bloodshed to a sure ditch. Simply perish from every unregistered weapon I had furbished."

As Quinn speaks to Kyle, Patrice in the kitchen overhears this. She feels reassured; if anything is to happen to Quinn, Kyle still wouldn't join up with the derelicts. Especially since his 13th birthday is on emergence. She thinks to herself, *Kyle is so fortunate to have a good father, along with an inheritance.*

As Kyle takes his shoes off and runs, Quinn says, "Hurry up and make sure you wash your hands."

Patrice, with a huge smile, hugs Quinn and says, "I'm lucky to have you as my man."

Quinn hugs Patrice and says, "I sincerely love our union. Oh and you're wearing my favorite perfume, hon."

Right now Rich is knocking down shots in an attempt to control his aggression. He's at one of his favorite bars called Wesson's. He thinks to himself. *When depression sets in, it's no question. It makes angry, drunk, doped up pedestrians wind up at police districts with bloody weapons and vengeful confessions. Close inspections reveal I'm ignoring moral lessons. I'm not trying to be a Christian or a Muslim like those in Bangladesh. Again and again at times I bang the desk again. Leave out the crib, the bar is where I'll take my step in. My guess is after I get tore down, I'll go home and get some rest then. Worries of tomorrow, bump it. My soon to be unconscious state will temporarily be anxiety and stress end.*

Rich then notices an acquaintance's reflection in a mirror. The dude's name is Haneef. He greets Rich, "It's been a long time, brother. You trying to drink away your problems chief?"

Rich smiles and says, "Man, my vision is distorted. Yo, to the bar by stress I was escorted, to drink some poison that I ordered." Then Rich asks, "Yo, you don't drink. Why are you here?"

Rich's question, Haneef ignores it. He turns his attention toward the bartender and tells him, "Hey, hold off right now. Don't pour it." Then turns back to Rich and says, "Look, this drinking interruption, I know you're not for it. But it's my duty, brother, to drop some healing facts. Don't let this world of spiritual anthrax play you out like a sax. It's no time for third eye cataracts. Be strong, one of the righteous inhabitants. Wise told me to holler at you, now what you so mad at?"

Rich blurts it, asserts it, "The day of judgment won't be averted. People ways are too perverted. All of this stress, I don't deserve it, or do I? One thing for sure, my businesses and responsibilities I won't shirk it. Honestly, much of the time I know I'm a jerk. Shit, and I'm worldly perverted."

Haneef points out, "Acknowledgement is great, however, don't beat yourself up. You're in the wrong state of mind to be intoxicating yourself—with that cognac off the shelf. I don't want to see you blow up like a stealth."

Rich belches, then says, "I know getting drunk won't help my wealth, neither my health. It's definitely better than me putting heat to somebody else for something small as an elf. When I look in the mirror, I see myself becoming sinful more quicker. Yeah, that's the picture—because what's making me happy is proof that I'm spiritually sicker. When times get bad, some so-called friends snicker as they consume liquor. Stop speaking to yah or look at you when you're down, then kick yah. No need to bicker. Let's see how my haters act when these fat pockets get even thicker. I refuse to be a loser. I'm a winner. I want to be successful, but for right now, I'm a stressful beginner. I'm no longer hustling. I'm striving hard to be upright in a world designed to keep me uptight—and up all night. I'm living in the valley of darkness, trying to find enough light."

Haneef says, "Right, for me Islam is the light. Islam is the sun. Allah is sufficient and beneficent. To be specific, it's your life. Stay with it. Don't diss it. Do you need assistance? Must I mention it? A worldly lifestyle will kill you like barbiturates. This isn't politics. It's a matter of life or death. We're not constituents."

Rich gets another shot to knock down and says, "At times I get sick with this. Man, it really hurts. It irks to see kids catch holes like cheap shirts. It comes down to who gets to the heat first. Let me take a leak first. Then we can continue the convo and get it on, bro, 'cause words of wisdom I thirst. The devil's power works from side to side, front and back, it lurks."

After about five minutes in the lavatory, Rich comes out and sits down beside Haneef and continues, "I got mad worries, sad stories. To-night stress really had it in for me. My mind needs to be immersed. I can't continue to chase the bottle and skirts. Then later hit the mosque or the church. My mind is dirty. I need to be brainwashed with the truth of the universe. I'm soon to curse before I burst."

As a sexy chick flirts, Haneef blurts, "You don't need to be coerced. You need a spiritual nurse, not something temporary and false. Get a natural high, God's upliftment. It's a gift, kid. Don't risk it. You want to experience inner calm. For me, it is Islam. For you, might be something else, don't qualm. Faith is vital to your productive development. Yes, it's relevant. Remember, Rich, sleep time is over. It's too many asleep and not enough soldiers. Time's getting colder. Try to expand on being sober. If you let it, the world, it will hold yah and before you know it, you're bowing to your lower. Sleep time is over. Rich, until next time, peace."

As soon as Haneef leaves, Rich tells the bartender, "Two more shots, please."

Wise arrives at Wesson's 20 minutes later. He greets Rich, "Tired of being a fool." Then he calls over a waiter. He places an order, then turns to Rich. "You're the main reason for your inner torture. Haneef's brother was killed over eight years ago somewhere in town, yet that brother somehow turned his life around. He made a serious rebound. He doesn't walk around with anger that's misplaced. The drugs have been replaced or erased. God is his center now. He's living proof that his brother's death didn't go to waste. He used his brother's death as a point in time to disrespect, then reflect, correct, and finally resurrect—his life. I talked to Quinn earlier. I knew you would wind up here for surely, sir. Look, Haneef, Grands, myself, and a few other cats we know are working on building community centers. One of them should be up and running by late winter. I would like you to be a part of this." Wise turns his head sharply and said, "Good, here's my dinner."

Wise begins to eat, however, he's cognizant of the fact that Rich hasn't responded, as he readjusts himself in his seat.

Rich takes his sunglasses off and states, "The community can kiss the shit that comes out of my ass. Yo, right now I wouldn't be part of any plans with Grands." Rich then crosses his arms and makes a tight fist with both of his hands.

After Wise eats a couple of wings and drinks some of his ginger ale, he looks at Rich, "Grands is offering his help, whether he does or doesn't. I refuse to fail. I will prevail. I know I can't change the world. I just want to implement intervention in this hell. You don't want to be a part of it, oh well. Your current mentality isn't too far from what we used to be. You know, the excessive drugs, guns, and women will sooner than later take you out, G. Gangs, in general, ours back in the day included. They serve as an apparatus for young men removal. Regardless where the gang is at, here in the states or in another country, senseless violence occurs entirely too much, G. I'm still a gangster. I make my own mark, despite the boundaries. The most high light and insight for the right plight has finally found me. Much of this crap in the streets is strategic, systematic genocide. Dudes from crews who's admired keeps peeps blazed up, maced up, caged up. Now my third eye peers through the maze, unhazed up. I give praise to the most high. I've changed my ways up. It's strategic, systematic genocide. Dudes from crews who'se admired—keeps people raged up. No longer is my coke and weed laced up. I used to have an unswitched brain which remained stuck, from the setup. I got fed up. Life, at times, seems as though it won't let up. Yet, I get up. Strategic combat is everywhere, fact. Ponder that. I honor facts, not deceptive tricks. Embrace the rhythm of life like receptive kicks and snares. Words of life punctures spirits. Some people will user to hear it. Plus, mentally I've crushed mimic—programmed activities, with a truth deeper than H2O, which flows through aqueducts. Who rocks with us? Knowledgeable cats who are insubordinate—like Haneef. You should adore it. Mentally begin recording it. The wrath of God these devils can't war with. Yes, it's the type of vision that gets me activated quick, for a people that's so sick. They walk around stinking. That ain't slick. Unawareness and ignorance leaves the threshold open to redundant, destructive madness. The saddest, baddest fad, yes. Self-esteem drops quicker than the property value in any impoverished address. The power is within to stop the sadistical, habitual, trivial, ungodly rituals. Until then, the pistol's pulled. Actually, it's insanity. Drastically, savagery, assault and battery with full capacity, along with rounds to the chest cavity. Simultaneously leaves victims in agony, pulled to the ground by the force of gravity. What audacity. Yes, now the forces I use to run with are mad at me. They're radically wiping us out with a scientifical strategy."

Wise pauses long enough to knock off a couple of wings and drink some more ginger ale. Rich halfheartedly listens as he observes a phat piece of tail he would like to nail.

Wise picks back up, "Some thugs want their coke and heroin to sell out. Make their fortune, then bail out. Platinum iced out jewels, son. Most of them are disillusioned. The proof, son, is in institutions—that house thousands of hustlers' ambitions, imaginations, and infatuations of fast cash making. Lonely sisters turn to each other. Lovers of the same sex and it captures, some brothers in jail who become banana slappers. Man, it's too many cats on a programmed level. Now I'm a different type of rebel. I'm talking about being conscious. To be honest, a lot of peeps rather be unconscious. You're not astonished. My force-field alienates me from the influential garbage. Sick messages, profanity, insanity, twisted vanity, in the entertainment arena has become adjacent. We shouldn't be so damn complacent. That's my statement. Face it. We can blaze one another, but when it calls for it, can we blaze the other? The real enemies who have us going out like suckers. Most of us are materialistic, pacified motherfuckers. Cats exposing their entire ass, underwear. Brains, is some there? Dirty, uncombed tons of hair. Father's son's lungs tear— from guns that flare, usually over something ridiculous. Their elders are sick with this. Hell, I bear witness to this."

Wise pauses again to finish the rest of his drink and food. Rich's demeanor has changed slightly. He's in more of a relaxed mood. Now he's finally recognizing the changes in his dude.

Wise concludes, "Ignorant, magnetic persuasion has young brothers decaying. It's Satan's methodical, spiritual perpetration and glorification of an ill situation. Lack of love has people getting blasted away, and— I'm not playing, when I'm saying that these governments aren't staying. Genocide is paying the price for not immediately escaping and praying. The righteous want deportation for your information. When I stand in front of the youth and commence the oration—for the permitted duration, I have 'em gazing from the power of my delivery in my narration. At any location that features me, youngsters eagerly, frequently be seeking me—for the serious frequency. My worldly, incompliant brothers speak to me—because I get deep as astronomy—or the real cats who control the economy. The hell with punks who wanna do wrong to me. Qualm with me. Ninety-five percent of them are cons to me. I live my life how I want it to be. I'm the opposite. I'm obstinate—to those on to me. My verbal illustration spills creation and chills frustration from the perpetual rhetorical, thugged-out firms, snakes, and worms. Spiritual germs who spark a surge. Rich, stop fucking around and get on some intelligent, grown man terms."

THE BASEMENT

It's 9:20. Quinn tells his wife, "Patrice, I'll see you later, honey." He then kisses his spouse, leaves out the door, and dips to Wise's house. Upon arrival, to Quinn's surprise, he notices Rich's fiery demeanor has been doused.

Rich announces, "So I see you decided to bounce. Come on, we're in the basement. Dog, I smell you. You gotta serious ounce."

As both of them make their way downstairs, Quinn pulls out his weed. Wise sees it and said jokingly, "Yes, indeed, just what we need. Mo weed."

Quinn gives Wise dap, then commences to prepare his blunt on his own lap. "Rich, me and Wise are tired of your crap. I must admit, I'm glad to see that you are much calmer now than earlier this evening."

Wise jumps in, "Yeah, right now we're just smoking and drinking. Just venting about what we're thinking." Wise pauses for just a moment to take his blunt and inhale. Then he exhales and continues, "Fellas, well, well. in a short time span we've seen the towers fall. Mass blackouts, hurricanes, earthquakes, and mad snowstorms. I know God and Satan are looking down like, yeah, we got more for 'em. The youth in the streets is my forum. Examining the data, I ponder if a new people were to rebuild a different world. Would it be a cycle of a different type of fucked up? Is it the nature of man or mankind? I don't know, neither do ya'll. I'll hush up. The question still remains, people, what's up?"

Rich takes a few more sips of his cognac and says, "Clowns try to work my nerves. They got mad words until I got mad with my verbs. I live my life staying to myself. It helps to sustain and maintain my wealth and health. Sometimes death is dealt from the very people you're trying to help. Wise, I know lately you've been talking to the troubled youth. You're trying to get them on the right track. Alright, I'll respect that, just watch your back. Devilish ways gots me staying selfish these days—in a world that's backwards and corrupt. Wise, I remember you told me, maybe I should go back to church. Sir, what? It didn't save me when I was younger, and it definitely won't now that I'm older. I'm opening up to you like a folder. I'm not moving weight anymore, however, my heart is colder. Shit, the biggest culprit is possibly behind the pulpit. His lifestyle, hypocritical bullshit. A religious hustler taking in the wealth for self. He could be molesting little boys as he's peddling heaven. A real parent would introduce him to the three fifty seven. In front of the congregation—for his ways of Satan. I would love to hold Satan. Beat 'em down along with the priest who be faking. Yeah, in front of their fokes shaking. Then leave 'em, bloody, dead, not pulsating. Ask God, why you let it happen in the first place? Yeah, the bullshit I'm hating. Yo, my dudes, I'm just stating—for every answer I get, I get another question. This be, in part, the reason for my many transgressions."

Quinn exhales smoke, then speaks, "Yo, in regard to religion, listen. You shouldn't let the deviant actions of some be the deciding factor on whether or not a faith in specific is beneficial. Followers of anything, good or bad, are going to screw up. That's official."

Wise agrees, "Quinn, I couldn't have said that any better, however, Rich, don't be so easy to let someone pull your lever. Hold yourself together. No man or woman has all the answers in the existence. Rich, I'm with you to a point. These religious fanatics can keep their distance. The hell with the inconsistent shit that's been done and written. I ain't kidding. Also that Satanic horse shit. I'm trying to stay on a successful course, kid. I have an Islamic spiritual base, however, I'm not a Muslim. I'm a conscious human being with strong views, which you hear in my distaste. This isn't Mecca. I don't make Salat every day. It's the belly of the beast. Yes, I submit and must admit at times I pray. Lately I've been doing my best to stay on point mostly. My life is real, not phony like those daytime soaps be. Quinn, my homey, pass me the VSOP. I'mma light unto myself and the wisdom I've gained, I've held it closely. Positively, I know I can't always be positive. Yet when I mentor, they listen to the knowledge I give. It might spark a few brain cells that been silence and unlived."

Rich has just received a text: "It's Kathy. I want to know when I will c u next."

Rich also realizes he is supposed to get up with Tracey and Stacey. Twins, two dimes he was going to hang out with tonight. Rich thinks to himself, *Not tonight. I'm not in the mood to be around a lot of people and lights.*

Quinn interrupts Rich's train of thought with, "My dude, the reason why you're so mad is because you feel like Melvin personally made you look bad. Melvin isn't you, and you're not Melvin. Watch yourself, son. It's mad ways to get hurt out here that can put you at unease. Mad ways to die, whether it by the knife, gun, or disease. Mad ways to die, mad ways to live. Watch your deeds. Rich, watch your deeds."

Rich remarks, "I'm smoking a weeded cigar. Drinking and thinking is it all a test, dig. I'm pondering verbally affairs, like F it. I'm lounging with ya'll, getting bent. I'm seriously thinking about who I'm gonna screw or what asshole I wanna pay back. I'm not talking about rent. Some cats need to be removed like lint—because their determined to be a pain in the ass. It's as if they can't help it. They wanna be like the last insane ass, who caught death, which came in a flash. Quinn, at times you make me feel as if you're trying to examine me. Trust me, I'm trying to not lose my sanity, but fools wanna stress it, vex it, F it. Here's my detonator button, assholes. Press it. Yeah, I'll lay a bastard out on the asphalt. I'm not waiting around to explain to the law how the ass asked for it. Cops wanna lock me down or see me shot down. Bastards wanna take my life. I analyzed the daily sights. Who's really living right—in a world that's governed wrong? As everyone else, I carry on—before I get buried. Darn—shit, I mean cremated. Wise and Quinn, half of our team faded. Now I sit here a part time introvert. My personal problems at times, I've downplayed it. How does that sound for me, crazy, no what? I got to say it. Getting my businesses afloat was crucial. Demons trying to stop my shine as usual, however, I refuse to—lose to—adverse circumstances. Strategically, I work through the madness. I used to kill 40s of steel. When I get horny, I drill in shorties that's real. Too many cats in the game who's corny and unreal."

Quinn interjects, "Goddamn dog! Must you stay on this 24/7 tough Tony shit? Look, we your peeps. My man, we know you're not on some bluff, phony shit. Yo, we don't wanna hear about who you want to bone or about you putting two in somebody's dome with the chrome. Come on, man. Leave that banging the hammer talk alone."

Rich shrugs his shoulders at Quinn. Then he looks at Wise and adds, "Ya'll have seein' me lay an asshole out and be the reason why he's on a gurney. Then turn around and beat the case with my attorney."

Wise cuts in, "You need to learn, G. You never know when it might be your turn. See, real gangsters keep their cool. They use their brains. That's how you really profit from your gains. Yeah, and that attorney's name is Raymon. You probably should hang around him more. Maybe then—you wouldn't act so damn immature. Rich, when it comes to getting money, you vigorously pursue it. I'm telling you, dog. Stop walking around here as if you're excluded. Put money in the pot for schools and programs. The kids deserve a better shot. Life has a way of making some remember when they thought they forgot. Look, Rich, I'm talking to you straight from the heart. Don't be like Len and catch one in the dark by some chick who set him up in the park."

Rich raises his voice towards Wise, "Nobody, I mean, nobody is taking my goodwill for being weak! I'm heaven and hell sent. I'll kick somebody's tail, bent! Me, you, and Quinn got on some kill, shit! We blasted that bitch up and her man. We left them wrecked like a major train derailment! I stay on some real shit!" Rich pours himself another glass and staggers over to a window. Then he utters, "I don't want to talk about my brother. It's that plain and simple."

Quinn exhales smoke and once again speaks. "Your brother is in a better place. We got to be ready to kill, but we shouldn't live to kill like Leatherface. That big drug dealer dream we used to embrace, lets never chase. We now operate on a legal go getter, clever pace." Quinn then turns his attention to Wise. "It's easy to become enraged these days. The streets can have any of us taken out in a blaze. You got to—we got to—be more careful in this maze. I wish I could change the ways. Erase plagues and AIDS. Kids are taught to get straight A's. It pays. Most won't no hooray, OK. Except for those in power who invest to dumb us up, so it's easy to sum us up. Slum us up and eventually numb us up. Systematically, powers that be disables much of the underprivileged come up."

Wise adds, "You right. It's so damn blatant. That's why when I'm not working, I rather read and smoke in my basement."

Quinn scratches his head, then says, "I feel you. I'm doing my best to go straight, but if anybody touches my kid or my soul-mate, I'll make his spirit relocate." Quinn pours himself a glass of cognac. Then he turns his attention to Rich and asks, "Yo, what you see outside? Whatcha eyeing at?"

Rich walks back over toward Quinn and Wise, then sits on the couch. He strokes his beard, then says, "I'm about to be out. I need to go home, man. Quinn, I'm just really bent. I'm zoning. I feel like somebody's watching me. I'm a little paranoid. Powell and Morris, I need to avoid."

Wise taps Rich's shoulder and says, "It'll be alright, soldier. I'll smooth everything over. Don't worry about Grands' boys. They won't come for you with the heavy toys."

Rich stands back up in a defensive posture. "I'm an asshole executer—who stays on point like sharpshooters. I rock popped Rugers, especially at cats who wanna be stressing me, pressing me, distressing me, and testing me. Trust me, you have seen the worst and best of me. Investments, my destiny. Enemies will be destroyed indefinitely. Two middle fingers to any pigs or haters who wanna question me. I have integrity. My businesses plus street savvy is part of my recipe. I knock chicks off alphabetically with unseen powers, such as mental telepathy. I'm just unquestionably blessed, you see, genetically. I have the flyest of accessories, which are impeccable to me. I move with the shakers and bakers. That's why the pigs are upset with me. They're pathetic to me, like fake gangsters that are synthetic to me."

Quinn yawns, then says, "Please, stop stroking yourself rhetorically. It's horribly boring to me."

Rich laughs, "Quinn, surely I will take that as my cue to leave accordingly."

They give each other a fist bump. Then Quinn and Rich go outside to get in their rides. "Hey, drive with some sense!" yells Wise.

COPS DIALOGUE

Right now it's a little past midnight. Powell and Morris converse inside a parked car, underneath a dim light. The nature of the discussion involves their condemned, grim life. Morris is deep sleep deprived. His anger and frustration is the only reason why he seems to be awake or alive.

"I'm so fucking tired of these serpents, these fucking vermins. I hate these belligerent degenerates with their fucked up sentiments, resentments, and contentments. Anything from accidental bumps or rubs to rival thugs has jugs looking like shattered light bulbs in front of nightclubs. Some bystanders watch and love the sight of assholes busting shots at each other late at night. Soon to be running from red and blue lights. It reinforces certain agencies' arguments to take away citizens' rights. Daily sights of buck wild, foul juveniles profiles, with crime records longer than the Nile, who know nothing but crack vials and clothing styles. They be on the chase from us, with our glock 17s. Excuse me, 40 calibers we unleashed in misdirected teens' spleens. It's all there to be seen -on the news. That pisses off and gives their elders the blues. Economic strain shouldn't have families ripped apart by genocide, suffering, and pain. Blow, blow, blow never seems to go out of style. Life has ups and downs like eyelashes. Thugs are agitated by us like rashes. We lock 'em up by the batches. Then the courts screw us. They let 'em back out to burn up someone else like matches. More bodies left on the street like ashes. Clashes with rival fools leaves assholes blown apart like bullseyes by rifles or tools. Bodies in this city drop more than bird shit does on the hoods of transportation. You know what, Powell, I need to put in for a fucking vacation. I guess what I'm saying is, I feel like we're spinning wheels. We chased down an asshole earlier today fueled with social ills. We chased that motherfucker up to speeds of 95 miles per hour on the interstate. We caught him with coke, weed, and stolen merchandise. I wouldn't be surprised if some loophole gives his ass a break. I do my job to the utmost technical precision, not unethical decisions. Shit, man! How many fucking times has the judicial system given my testicles a kicking!"

Powell says, "I'll be sincere with this. It's easy to feel despair, yes. The system needs to be repaired, yes. Morris, hear this, we can't get careless. We must always practice fairness. These street punks are killing each other for money. It's either that or getting locked up for illegally making money. I remember one dealer's excuse was his daughter was hungry and crummy, plus the stress had him crying with his nose runny. These guys comrades are getting put in body bags for bags of contraband on this stolen land. Man, so many souls are lost daily in the streets -for trying to survive in this beast. It seems as if hell gots us all for keeps. How many dudes we've rolled up on with their frame leaking on the sidewalk? For jive talk their brain leaking. Maybe I'm just a cop insane speaking. Yeah, my man, a lot of crime. A lot of grime. A lot on my mind. I really hope I have a lot of time. I'm really just trying to finish my shift without having my chest cavity becoming void. Bullets have no name on them when they are deployed. Sons' and daughters' blood is dripping. The clock is always ticking. What's the solution? What the fuck are we missing? Oh, not to mention, how about the countless fools who can't cope with life's crap? Those who's weak turn to dope or crack. How do we solve that? You know what, we can't. We adapt. Retirement isn't paradise, however, I look forward to it before my time is gone off the map."

Powell finishes off his cheap scotch, then tosses it across the parking lot. It shatters against some sharp rocks. Morris finishes off his gin. He tosses his bottle out of the car and comes again. "Our local government tells us the city is broke. Maybe that's because the politicians are too busy giving themselves raises and stealing money. It's a fucking joke! Yeah, we're both depressed and stressed by the glorification of popping nines. One of the many reasons why so many catch early flat lines. Minds are cluttered with senseless violence, sexism, and materialism that gets them destined for prison. The system is the slave master's whip. Wisdom is what so many of us need, but 24/7 on the radio, big booties, coke, and weed. Crime rising, hard to survive and—dying everywhere like liquor advertising. Politicians denying—the truth is wide, yes, as ignorance develops, quicker than laboratories, develop a new virus. Revolvers and semi-automatic weapons are being gripped. Man, many of the assholes doing the tripping don't give a damn about going to prison. Somewhere down the line, their vision was tarnished. They took a moral nuclear bomb hit. Thoughts of some of the shit I've seen makes me wanna vomit. Most of us are screwed by economics. Darn it, the people who run this world are demonic. It's too much poisonous venom instead of wisdom. It would behoove us all to be rid of third eye astigmatism. Work on inner criticism—and strive for a righteous vision. Now I'm turning on some music so I can listen to some R&B rhythms."

Powell scratches his dome. Then he let it be known, "Yeah, it's been a long day and a long night. Time to go home, right? Needless to say, we had a very productive day. Richard Conoway doesn't even know he's going to help us put Grands away."

10

SO DAMN FINE (A DIME)

Right now Rich is smiling as he's driving, due to the compliments that's been piling. A chick by the name of Sylvia decides to give him a dial, and she's wanted him ever since she's laid eyes on him.

"Sylvia, I wanna peel yah. I wanna feel yah and drill in yah. Then maybe chill wit yah," Rich says, as he envisioned both of them in bed. Himself on his back and her on top kissing his head.

Sylvia, in a sexy voice, "Rich, you speak so forward. It's unexpected, yet excellent. Well now, since you said it, why don't you come, oooh yes, and get it. I'm all alone in my hot tub. I made lasagna earlier today and I still got some. I would like you to come over only if you really, really wanna."

Rich thinks to himself, *She's hot as a sauna. Her Italian Ass wants me to beat up that vagina. She's been on me since Melvin fixed her Honda.* "You know what, sexy. I'm gonna."

She gives him her address. She isn't too far out of the way. He is glad, yes. Within 15 minutes flat, Rich makes it to where she is at. He makes it there for the allure. The time is 12:54. When Sylvia opens the door, he proclaims, "I'm going to break your back like the law." He snatches off her bath towel. Then he sexually bangs out her wet body on her floor; to the point where her core is sore. She screams at times as if her insides are tore. Rich hammers away at her, grabbing her by the throat. He is enjoying another late night score.

For Rich, this isn't impractical. At times he is sexually radical and/or tactical. As he sucks on her nipples and clavicle, he proclaims, "You love the way my nuts be slapping you and the way my pipe be impacting you." Her orgasm confirms it is all factual as her moistness intensifies around her vaginal.

Another night has passed. Rich enjoys smashing Sylvia's ass. She gives him a plate to take home the following morning before he makes a dash.

When Rich makes it home, he notices he has a message on his phone. It is Yvette. "You are hard to get. Your phone must be off. I've been trying to reach you, shit. Guess who dropped by the salon today. She wants you to meet her tomorrow, Sunday. She told us girls she would like to see you around one. She didn't tell us where. You should and would know the place, hon. She's in town visiting her mom, really. She's still very pretty. I'm talking about Jaclyn Gomez. I know you're wondering. She's still phat with a huge rack, man, oh yes."

The message has ended. Rich falls into his couch with his mind suspended. Everything in his life is of no existence. He closes his eyes to be engulfed by a reminiscence of the first time he saw Jackie at a distance.

Wooo, you got a brother staring, glaring. I ain't caring. Your skin complexion is smooth and fare, and—I wish we were a pair, damn. On top of that, what you're wearing is sensual. It tends to pull my attention. You need to know my intensions. My mind is in suspension. I must mention the way you walk with a switch and…I'm feeling an extension. Look at what I'm missin'. It's not a dream, 'cause myself I'm pinching. Steady sipping—the Remy Martin. I want you for more than just a friend for talking. Emotions and intense passion is in me sparking. I got to step to you before you depart. About you, I'm trying to receive memory lost. My visual is off. If I don't say something soon, misery is the cost. Up until now, my vision was 20/20. Now it's blow, blam, bam. Oh honey! Honey! Your beautiful good looks stunned me. I hope you won't shun me. As I walk past, I'm captivated and fascinated by your elegance and presence, you have dead presidents. I wanna hit your residence. You flex intelligence, proper table etiquette. I hear you laughing with your girlfriend, gossipy type rhetoric. At times I can be funny, just to see you crack that gorgeous smile. I would act silly as a child. Baby, only if you knew the attraction I'm packing. I truly hope I get the proper reaction. It's scary. My inner thoughts, only if you could hear me. You would become weary. You wouldn't want to come near me. Then again, maybe you would be flattered and help steer me—over to you with a wink and—if I could, I would get on one knee and start singing. Hoping for your clinging and some mingling. Forget the martini, and I would have you tingling. I'm tired of lingering. You just ate two plates full in a little time, yet still graceful. Turn around again so I can see your cleavage and face, cool. I can't believe this. Those beautiful eyes, lips, hips, and thighs. As I analyze hypnotized, tantalized, with a rise to no surprise. You dissed guys—who were suckers. No realness or style, just tacky. I caught your girl calling you Jackie. I wish you would sit on my lap. See, so I could whisper soft, hot erotic things to make you squirm. For you, my desire yearns. If me and you were together, you would be my number 1 concern. I would keep the relationship firm. Super long term. Damn, darlin', you're fabulous. You give me a rush. You're so fine, I would make you blush. The sound of your voice quiets me. From me, no fuss. I would hush. I know, a little exaggerated, but I would love you too too much. You make me wanna bust. I want you in my clutch. Look at those nice, bulging cups. I wanna undress you and make extraordinary love with you. Sex you. Sugar, you're fantastic. Your radiance, I can't get past it. Me and you should become passionate. You have such beautiful facial bone structure. I wanna FU emmmmm. I need to touch yah. You're one of the world's greatest wonders. I don't want another. A monogamous relationship. One on one. I'm stepping to you, lover.

Rich picks himself up off his couch. He has just under an hour to take a shower, get himself together before he bounce. He's overjoyed to see Jackie again. It's been years. When she moved away, Rich wouldn't admit it, but he shed many tears.

As Rich drives to the destination with no hesitation, he thinks to himself, *Now out of the blue, she wants to meet me at Bliss, the restaurant we first met at. We used to eat there a lot. It was her favorite. I'll never forget.*

It's now 12:59. Rich sees Jackie sitting by herself at a table sipping a glass of wine. He notices right away she looks so fine and still blows his mind.

They both give each other a tight embrace and get caught up on each-others' lives, as if there is no time to waste. They talked for over an hour and a half. As both of them sip from their own glass, they are unaware of how much time has passed.

After they finish eating, Rich stares at Jackie and says, "You gotta believe me."

Jackie states, "Please, don't try to deceive me."

Rich comes again, "Look, I mean it. I want to continue what we got going on this evening. Please, don't deny me. I see the way you're still eyeing me. You know you'll have a fun time with me."

Jackie responds, "I don't know if you're the guy for me. Yeah, you're beautiful. I love your face and the feel of your body to me. Yes, you inside of me. I love charisma. You are ambitious. I love many of your qualities. Your hair is reminiscent of a tsunami to me. Yes, I would love it if you would make me a mommy to be. Come on though, let's be real. Don't lie to me. The street life, you can't give it up. That's, in part, why I moved to Raleigh. I don't want my heart to hurt because some animal put you down on the dirt. That's why I moved away and engulfed myself in my work. I'm only here for a few days. My mother isn't well. Here's my card if you want. You can reach me on my cell. I'm glad to see that you're doing well. You're looking swell, still handsome as hell."

Rich says, "I'll be staying in touch. Despite what you think, I've changed a bunch. Lately I've been an ass. Yes, I've been in the dumps. I lost a close friend. That's life—gotta deal with the humps and the bumps. I know you're in a bit of a rush. I'll be calling you soon."

Jackie smiles and says, "I had a hunch."

They both hug and wave each other off. The love is still strong. They are surprised that after several years, it isn't gone. As she steps away, Rich thinks to himself, *that woman still takes my breath away.*

Before she gets too far away, Rich quickly says, "Hey! Let me escort you to your SUV. Here's my number. Call me in a couple of hours. I would like to prepare dinner for just you and me. Don't refuse me. I'll keep you enthused, please. I'm a better gentleman now. I'm being truthfully."

Jackie is shocked. "Oh my! You would cook for me?

Rich says, "Absolutely. You are the love of my life. That's what you be to me, cutie."

Three hours have passed. When Jackie arrives, Rich greets her. "Time moves fast. I'm glad you made it to my house, at last. I made us a nice four course meal. I just wanted to spend some quiet time with you to let you know how I feel. I'm keeping it 100. I'm keeping it real. I want us to be a couple again. I'm ready to chill."

Jackie, with a smile, shakes her head and says, "You don't waste any time. Why should I believe you this time? Wow, by the way, your place and the meal look fine."

Rich retorts, "Thanks for being kind. Jackie, trust me, I've learned from my mistakes. I'm a little older now. I move at a different pace. Look, before we talk any further, let's sit down. Let's say grace. Tell me how dinner taste."

After making light talk over dinner, Rich confesses, "When you left, my heart felt pain. It hurt me like a splinter. This needs to be asserted. It wasn't inadvertent—that we were one hell of a couple. It was apparent. I want it to be that way again, except better, for certain. I don't take you for granted or a plaything. I want us to once again become intimate and share our sentiments. Maybe I'll slide on a ring on you as I'm amazed by your elegance. I'm telling this, the communication saves us the unneeded altercations. My inclination is to keep the emotional embracing—that we got between you and me. Unity—gots me feeling lovely when you rub me—the right way, night or day. When you give me a massage, I feel like a king on a throne who's not alone, living mad large. I'm trying to be fully honest. Don't be astonished. You're my goddess. All of my dumb street recklessness has been admonished. I've deserted the carnage and the garbage. No more ménages. I would never cheat on you. That would be more criminal than espionage shits. Jackie, me and you will go on an expedition and love each other's disposition as we are kissing. You'll listen to the sound of the sea, sure. They'll be more times like that when I'll take you on excursions. No need for searching—cause this brother is satisfied. I fantasize as I gaze into your eyes. I recognize more of this will never be enough. You sent me through an inner self metamorpho-

sis. Of course, it's hard when we're both moody. Your love will never re-
fute me. Even when times get rocky or wilder than zoology. Our love is
more solid than the subject of lithology. Apologies are traded cause I feel
for you, you feel for me. Our fidelity and will see, will prove skepticism
wrong. Our love stands firm. It stands strong. Now I want you to spend
the night. You feel what I feel, now it's right. Tomorrow morning I'll serve
you strawberries, bananas, a side of trail mix. We'll discuss exotic trips
on sail ships. Impressing you, I'll never fail, miss."

Jackie is blown away in a zone she can't delay. She's prone to stay. She
grabs Rich's hands and says, "You are such a beautiful man. Now that
I'm in your presence, I feel I'm drowning in love, so intensely emotional.
You're my life preserver, and I want to stay afloat with you. Out of all your
women, I didn't know until now that I meant the most to you. I'm still
single. I work a lot and hate to mingle—in the dating scene too. Wow, I
mean wooo! My love for you is keen, too. This is unbelievable. I would
be remiss not to admit that you as my man is my wish. We are still in love
with each other, Rich."

Both engage in a deep, loving kiss. No woman other than Jackie has
been able to capture Rich's heart in her grips. This experience for Rich, is
unusual, nonetheless, a welcome twist.

M.P.R

Right now across town in a well-known boxing gym, Wise is speaking to some young brothers who will listen to him.

"We're living in a corrupt existence. Everything evilistic is propelled with persistence. For instance, cultural and spiritual well-being is based on material. From the time you wake up, even before the cereal, until night, when you're dome hits the pillow. It's my will, yo, to speak it. The truth, I'm on some deep wit, along with the street shit. I'm well heated. Everything is justified by the freaking dollar. Sin is in yo. Out the window with morals, Christ, or Allah. Talk about horror. Woe to those who don't fear God. You don't know what comes tomorrah. Are we living in the last days and then some? I think so, however, what's most significant is it's not all about the income. There's a war going on between good and evil. How can we prevail if our souls are for sale? If you have no solicitude about what you say or do, don't be surprised when directly or indirectly it comes right back to you. Violent glorification is a mechanism that stimulates a programmed nation. Emotional aberrations, abrasions degradation, genocidal brain waves, son, is a terrible ramification—from the B.S. that is taught to generations. My generalization is the apparatus of the enemy is mis-education. Yes, I feel infuriation. Ya'll really don't want to get me started on TV and the radio stations. It's a figment of your imagination—if you're in the public eye and claim not to be a role model. Your whole persona is hollow, is the equation. That's what I said. I'm simply saying, negative or positive is the only choice your voice has. Maybe even somewhere in between, when you're on the scene. I'm not trying to be an ass or come off foul. Yo, it takes a village to raise a child. That idealism was good back in the day and still is good now. Brothers, we need balance instead of the constant trash. Cats talk so much, shit, their mouths pass gas. I don't give a damn about a dude's cash he gots to flash. I care about truth and programs. Listen up and listen close. Especially for ya'll who have kids. Never lose your focus and hope. I'm telling you, never use that dope. There's more to life than it seems. Even for those in the slums catching crumbs and dead dreams. What does it mean? Life's about choices, faith, and how you raise your seeds. There's more to life. Without faith, money doesn't take away all the pain and strife. I'm maneuvering through the valley of death. The illest actions this day in time aren't that ridiculous. People who are indigenous—give up to the power structures. Many of them wind up with late night binges, syringes, and violent endings. Yes, on the flip side, the rich commit murder and suicide too. While the poor die in rival gang wars—at maximum speed. Rounds cause sisters and brothers to bleed. Lives are taken as quick as they breed. Seeds have no lead—except the same cycle. Jail or an early grave. Slaves in cages can't help their children in development stages. There's more to life than wages. I flip thoughts like pages. As myself ages, I see spiritual declination. Foul stimulation like taxation. This is fueled by the fast cash making. Followed by the fast way in the system. Shackled ligaments for those who, enmeshed in imprisonment, exist. Some inmates catch 'em stiff. As their ass parts more than a fool and his money. When in incarceration, mad altercations explode. Today fingerprints. Tomorrow bar codes. Nonfictional, just literal facts. Three meals and a snack brings 'em back to their holding facility. Here's the deal, see. About 40 grand, my man, is spent per individual. New jails are set up to house the remaining residuals – when overcrowding befalls. The system gots too many brothers by the balls. I've had many who told me that I was wasting my time trying to reach contaminated minds. Those who interpose when knowledge was disclosed became froze when the truth began to hose. I'm intolerant. I won't be stopped. Everyone who knows me knows I've changed. They acknowledge it. I want to help youngsters' development. I made my dollars, shit. I know when one regurgitates. I pull no breaks. I extirpate—the problem, for it's spiritual. I use my mind, soul, body to combat those who want to block me from releasing the youth from society's ills and grips, son. Proper faith and education is the prescription. Ya'll know about my street recognition. Listen, I know rockology and toxicology involving gangsters and fakes. I introspect and retrospect on present and past mistakes. I did what was necessary for me to turn my life around. We all must utilize our third eyes, so we can recognize the moves made on us in the dark, like the owl. Files and documents have been proven to be proficient, concerning coverups to make the masses mentally deficient. Young brothers, in my conclusion, get your mind, soul, and body right. You'll never lose, son. You'll experience inner peace, even in the beast. Knowledge and insight will cause wisdom to form. The brain is more powerful than a thunderstorm. Seek knowledge, for your brain, it won't become too immense. Deception will be rinsed. You'll rocket over a mind that is dense. Strive for omnipotence—among the poisonous, venomous resistance. Hood bafoonery should be defuncted and or punked. Spiritually, I'm on an enlightenment kick. I utilize wisdom and wit. My brain is fit, among the shit. I'm completely equipped. I've axed down egotism of imbeciles who were demented. My delivery, at times, can be eccentric, yet, the intent is to give the unlifted a lift quick. The upshot, 90 percent of the evildoers pitch a fit quick. They walk off on themselves. They quit. I perform CPR on brain cells. Why? Let me explain. Well, too many dudes are going down insane trails."

When Wise arrives home from the boxing gym, Felicia, his girl-friend, has a note and a plate waiting for him. The note says, "I know you are tired from boxing and running your mouth. Eat, take a shower, and turn the lights out. I want you to get some rest. After I finish visiting my sister, I want you at your best. You know what I'm talking about. I want to see your muscles flex. I want us to engage in hot, intense sex. Love you. No other man I put above you. Oh, by the way, I want to snuggle and hug too. ☺"

After Wise takes a shower and eats, he takes his tired body to bed. He closes his eyes and has a strange vision in his head.

He sees a split image of himself in a boxing ring. One image of himself is getting beat half to death by the other before the bell went, *ding, ding!* The image of himself, who has won the match, looks at the other and says, "Here's something you should grasp. You'll get steamed like kettles when I step on your ego like peddles. Your emotion can't simmer, neither settle, due to frustrations of a no win altercation. Sometimes it's recreation—when I'm demonstrating, the art of disintegrating. The power of Satan's rule over your spiritual network that exerts itself through your shell. Physically, mentally, and spiritually I repel—evil forces. Of course, it's dangerous, but I have an obligation to dispel—ideas of moral consciousness being weak and soft. Devils hear my words and walk off, or, like Van Gogh, take their ear off. I'm the man on any section of land, understand. I leave the foolish in a pitiful condition. Apprehension, example, a cat on smack. Decoding cats who front is easy. I have expertise in ethology, which is the study of animal behavior. It has similarities to your brain. Life can getcha insane. I refuse to crack like a picture frame. Watching your personality reveals your non-spirituality, which produces your rubbish. I guess you could replace rubbish with the word mythology. Especially if you think you can overpower me. Sociology gots you in need of psychiatry. Don't lie to me—and say I don't make sense, your sir mental impotence. To be more accurate, make a correct statement. Something like you can't comprehend. That I would agree upon, due to your mental chains within. You only know the norm, while I'm on another tip. The storms are getting worse. This world is cursed. The beast with blasphemy on its forehead thirsts for blood of many. Tent of skin, doesn't matter. It'll take any. Dry bones, you are a distant clone. M.P.R. will remove you from your throne. My mind, soul, and body are in unison with *maximum positive reinforcement.* The unstable, evil side of me will continue to get pummeled with no remorse. Shit."

SURPRISE

Monday morning, Jackie and Rich wake up energized as they lie in bed, gazing into each other's eyes. The night they had will forever be memorized. Rich gently grabs Jackie and says, "I hope what I'm about to say doesn't make you scared. I'm cutting back on my temper and getting impaired. Moments like this are meant to be continuously shared. Sincerely, it's true. I want to marry you."

A tear drifts across Jackie's overjoyed, smiling face. She says, "Ohh, yes." Then they give each other a tight, loving embrace. Rich adds, "Across the room over there, you see those pretty flowers in the vase. Give them to your mother from both of us when you go to her place."

After Rich prepares the small, tasty breakfast which he had promised, Jackie comments, "Honest, I really don't want to be leaving. I will return later this evening."

Rich remarks, "Well, I know where I'll be then."

Jackie leaves with the flowers. Rich quickly takes a shower. Then he gives Vince a call and tells him, "I'll be there in a half an hour."

Once Rich pulls up on the parking lot, Vince comes out of the shop. "Rich, it's a chick waiting to talk to you, who's smoking hot."

Rich is like, "Yo, who is she? What's she got?"

Vince says, "Yo, I think it's about some property. She's a fox, holler, G."

Rich and Vince walk inside. Off the top, Rich notices how fine she is, but his mind is tied to his future bride. He wants to stay true to Jackie and have nothing to hide. Rich, however, does pause to eyeball her pretty head down to her heels. He also notices instantly along with her looks and killer curves, she got bills. Her frame is curvy, yet petite. Her beauty is elite. Rich's sexual urge seems as though it won't retreat. The young lady stands up from her seat and walks toward Rich to greet. She extends her hand and in a Latino voice that's sweet, "You must be Richard Conoway. The one I've been waiting on to meet."

Rich knows he has never met this woman before, for sure. Her beauty is hard to ignore—like his inner sexual lion's roar. He confirms, "Yes, I be Mr. Conoway. Who might you be? What brings you this way?"

The beautiful woman states, "My name is Camilla Velez. I have property I must sell, yes. I'm not a realtor. My uncle died and left me property properly. I would love to show you the commercial property with lot, see. Proof of ownership I got, se."

Camilla hands Rich her folder with correct documentation. It seems that she does own the building and lot as she's been saying. After Rich finishes scanning over the papers, he's aware it looks to be pretty official. Rich looks back up toward Camilla and states, "I would like to make a copy of this, miss. Is it cool?"

Camilla answers, "Of course. Sure, Mr. Conoway. I really hope I will have the opportunity to show you the building today. I know you are a very busy man. Please don't turn me a way. Please, pretty please. OK?"

Rich tries his best not to give in to her looks, but the tone of her voice, her curves, and pretty brown eyes are more devastating than Wise's left hooks. When Rich finishes making copies for his friend Raymon to look at, he asks Camilla, "By the way, how did you happen to come this way? How do you know my name? Please say."

Camilla approaches Rich closely. "Everyone knows about you and your real estate interest. If you buy, I get to move West before winter flex. I should have told you when I introduced my...uh, how dumb of me. Excuse me. Hon, I have family in Houston. My uncle left me property worth a good amount of loot, hon. Now the time seems right for me to move out at once. As soon as I get some checks, I'm out West. Yes, I'm so stressed and pressed. Maybe if I had a guy like you to caress, I wouldn't be so eager to change my address."

Rich fights his inner self not to give into his sexual madness. "Miss Velez, you are welcome to read one of the magazines off the desk." Rich hurries away from Camilla and into the back of his shop. There he instructs Vince in front of the other mechanics that Vince is the one calling the shots.

"You are in charge now, since Melvin's head went pop. I don't – we don't – want business to drop or flop."

All the other mechanics respect Vince being in charge. It is easy for them to adopt. Vince has an extra confidence in his bop. Privately for a few minutes, Rich discusses Vince's payroll. Everything is good. Rich tells Vince, "Alright, I'll stop through tomorrow. Gotta roll."

When Rich arrives back out in front of the shop, Camilla gets off her cell. She asks, "Can I show you the building for sale?"

Rich answers, "Swell, what the hell?"

Outside Camilla tells him, "I really appreciate you taking the time and being so willing to see the building."

Rich glances at her cleavage and thinks, *Her blouse is too revealing. It's hard as hell to fight this feeling.* He takes a deep breath and tells her, "Umm, let me follow yah."

Camilla says, "You could ride with me, but OK. It's less than half an hour"

As she walks away looking very sexy in her business suit toward her BMW, Rich's mind is saying, *If Jackie wasn't in my life, within 24 hours I would have done you.*

It is a beautiful, clear, breezy, sunny fall day. Rich has his sunroof open as he followed Camilla on the way. On arrival, Rich thinks, *Everything looks OK. A nice, two-story building. Hey, structurally it looks straight as a laser ray.*

Both of them get out of their cars looking like movie stars. Camilla stands next to Rich and says, "The building has a security system and the windows have bars. It's a precaution even though this area is nice and pretty quaint. The building is straight. Are you ready for me to show you inside?"

Rich, with a detailed eye, answers, "I can't wait."

When they walk inside, Rich notices plenty of tables and chairs. "Oh, this used to be a restaurant here."

After they walk around, Camilla tells Rich, "There is more. Please don't make me implore. I would love to show you around upstairs to finish the tour—before you hit the door."

Rich agrees and goes up to the next floor to explore the décor. As soon as he takes a step up there, *Blam! Blam!*

"Fuck, yeah!" shouts Grands' number one muscle, whose name is Bully. He is commencing to give Rich an ass whipping fully. He grabs Rich and yells, "Did I astound yah? I'm going to continue to pound yah."

Bully two-pieces Rich and slams him on a counter. He punches him three times with a straight right. For Rich, it is good night. His ass is out. He blacks out. He continues to punch him as blood splashes about. He is almost mashed out.

Camilla takes out her switch blade and jams him with it. Then Bully takes a chair and slams him with it. Grands shouts, "Rich ass has submitted! Baby, goddamn ya'll are committed! Don't dead him!"

Grands observes Rich as he puffs his cigar and scratches his head. Bully, Camilla, and another guy named Hands smile as Rich bleeds. Another woman sitting in a dark corner says, "I'm going to enjoy Rich laying eyes on me before I put him permanently to bed."

A couple of moments later, Rich finds himself lying on the floor with his ankles and wrists duct taped. His face, head, and gut ache. His mouth and nose are bloody. His head feels as if it was used for rugby. Rich sits up and looks at Camilla. "Whore, why did you fuck me? Shit, my side! Who stuck me? Bully, you ah bitch! You snuck me!"

Hands suggests, "Rich, chill out before shorty here makes the rest of your blood spill out."

Camilla is sitting in a chair smoking a cigarette. She mentions, "Who would have figured it. I'm a bad bitch for getting mighty you in this predicament."

Bully is holding Rich's gun. "Look at you now, Mr. Smooth Rich. Punk ass, I broke you up like a toothpick. You got no tools to spit or recruitment. You soft like lubricant. You should've not come to the warehouse and got all brutally exuberant. You ah cat I used to be cool wit, but shit."

Rich blurts, "You got me. You got the drop on me. Go ahead and pop me. You still are a big ass bitch for stealing me. Yeah, for real, G. Come on, kill me!"

Grands walks over in front of Rich so he can be seen. "For me it's not personal. It's about the green. Know what I mean?"

Grands takes one of the chairs. He sits in it, then slides over closer to Rich as he strokes his facial hairs. He leans over close to Rich's face and blows smoke. Again he speaks, "Camilla is the one who gave you a poke. When she stuck you, it gave me a jolt. Isn't that funny? Laugh, Rich, even though it's not a joke."

Rich, in agony, struggles to point out, "All the times me and you used to hang out, now you set me up to be banged out. What's this thing about?"

Grands answers, "It's, in part, about a new and better coke connect. My connect wants you smashed. It's a bet. When you came to my warehouse and lost your head. Yeah, that's why my connect wants you offed, just dead. Yeah, you're thinking it's a shame, no doubt. Understand this, my ambition isn't to blame, concerning you being banged out. This nightmare right here is your doing. Let me be quite clear. That bullshit you pulled at the warehouse, I was going to let it slide. Dog, the chick in my ride felt different inside after listening to my dudes confide."

Grands pauses, puffs a couple of times, then continues. "I'm not tak-ing a loss. I'm the baddest boss. I'm not soft or false. You gotta pay the cost. You're about to be fried up like a cross, then tossed. It's business for me. My heart is frost. You don't have much time to exhaust. A better price and product is being imported for my customers who snort it—or bang it in condos, mansions, or crack houses that's boarded. Fuck it. They can smoke it as long as they can afford it. The greed, I absorb it. It won't be aborted. I gave a certain woman a personal tour, Rich. She wanted to see what I do. You know the sort of shit. You going off at the warehouse, she couldn't ignore the shit. You're not in the game anymore, Rich. I'm in it 100 percent—for the importance and the endurance. I helped out my new connect. It's insurance. Honestly, fuck this planet in orbit. I hope it goes up in flames like a torch, Rich. Life's a hardcore bitch. If I got to set you up for the sure hit, fuck it. I'm all for it. Sorry, dog, it's too great of a score, Rich. More money and power. I'm after that. You about to get blast at. I need the cash jack off the fast track. I'm a class act who doesn't want to be surpassed, fact. Life has ups and downs like the Nasdaq. I want this connect. You can grasp that. It's too good. That's that. You know me. None of what I said should traumatize yah. It's about the best supplier with the best product to get the fuckers higher."

Time is pending in regards to Rich's ending as his head is spinning. Grands, Hands, Camilla, and Bully are grinning. The other woman who has been sitting in a dark corner of the room all this time decides to make her presence felt and speak her mind.

YOU'RE DEAD

As the well-dressed woman stands up and walks closer to Rich, she pulls her long hair in a ponytail. Rich, battered and bruised, mumbles, "What the hell?" as his face becomes pale.

She asks, "Rich, do you have any questions for me, before I kill you shortly??

Rich, weak and in pain, forces out, "Rita, Rita, You're dead. You're not alive. What's going on? This doesn't jive."

The woman with a cold, mean expression and bottled-up aggression, calmly says, "I'm not dead. I'm half dead." She turns toward Grands and notes, "Those pits of yours in the basement haven't been fed." She then turns back toward Rich and says, "Who am I, mister? I'm Gina, Rita's twin sister. How does that get yah?"

Gina leans in close to Rich's face and spits in it. Camilla kicks him in it, then pulls out her knife again and sticks him with it. Rich screams, "Aaaaaaahhhhhhh!"

Gina adds, "You're in pain, good. This is what I've been waiting to see. Ever since you showed up at the warehouse on your pistol whipping spree."

Camilla interjects, "I agree."

Then Camilla gives Rich's face a knee. Gina sits in a chair and sparks a tree. Then she goes on to say, "Come on, loud mouth, talk to me. What's up? You seem to be speechless."

Rich utters, "I'm at my weakest. It's hard for me to speak, shit."

Gina points out, "Yeah, Bully did whip your ass like a horse in the Preakness."

Rich coughs and spits a little blood as he makes a mug. Bully laughs and says sarcastically, "My man, come on. Where is the love?"

Gina stares at Rich and goes on. "Me and my sister were alike in some ways. We also were unalike in some ways. My sister left Miami to get away from an abusive guy. She moved here to give her entrepreneurial savvy a try. Unfortunately she also hooked up with your boy. Now, in his defense, you wanna beat dudes up make bullets fly. Your friend, that turd, is the reason my sister is dead." Gina's eyes were becoming teary and red. "I can't believe she's gone. Why couldn't he let her go instead? Rita started talking to Chauncey initially to work out some sort of arrangement. I'm talking about some good, cocaine shit. Establish a real profitable domain, Rich. Your boy was like, no! He had to aim his shit. Bang his shit. He got on some slain shit. Now my family is in anguish. To my family, I had to explain this. When Chauncey and Rita became involved, Melvin shouldn't have been appalled. Their relationship had already dissolved. Their problems couldn't be resolved or solved. It was at the point where every day they brawled. Their marriage should've been annulled and her things should've been U-hauled. Thanks to Melvin, my sister's head by two rounds was installed. The upshot, her spirit was recalled. You'll pay for the way my sister was wronged! I'm thinking about ordering Bully to take you to the basement to be mauled. I told my brother Rico, who's locked down, that I would kill you myself and your death wouldn't be painless. For you, taking up for Melvin, I have much disdain, bitch. The way my cousin poked you with that knife, I know it still hurts." Gina unzips her purse.

Grands is like, "Yeah, baby. It's time he be faded. He's beaten, plus dehydrated."

Grands gives his jaws a pause to continue puffing. He walks over closer to Rich to get a better view of him in pain, grunting, and suffering. He then adds, "You really started something. You started some shit like Ex-Lax. Now you gotta be removed like cataracts. It's a matter of facts. Rich, listen, pay attention to my diction. It's not fiction. You caused this friction. I got a subscription on how to keep the latest firearms spitting without missing. I made the decision with the precision of a surgeon's incision to give Bully the permission to beat your ass into submission. I won't stand anyone or anything getting in the way of my ambition or cash addition addiction. I'm the reason for Gina's acquisition of ammunition in this jurisdiction."

Rich musters the little energy he has left to say, "So I see the new connect is too enticing. In this business, it's nothing nice, man. Hell, your explanation does suffice, man. Know this, if I wasn't fucked up, I would punch out your lights, Grands. Then I would take your life and run your ice, man. I'm just saying, you know my likes, man. I got stripes, Grands. I should've listened to my people's advice and now I gotta pay the price, damn."

Grands thinks to himself, *Rich, you really are taking this like a man. My dog, you really got guts. If you wasn't so damn foolish, you would've got touched.*

Gina stands up and kicks the chair. "It ends right here! I'mma show everyone here what my vengeance does to you. It's nothing else to discuss with you or fuss with you. I've had enough of you. It's time you feel what my grudge do. Fuck you! I'm going to feel one hell of a rush, fool, when my 45 bust you and permanently hush you. Fuck your rebuttal. Your body is going to make one hell of a puddle—as me and my cousin take off like a shuttle."

Hands yells, "You're not the only one who has a rush too! The fuzz too! I just buzz 'em through!"

Grands yells, "What, you! I trusted you! I'm gonna snuff you!"

He pulls out as four cops, Morris, Powell, plus two, bust through and shove Grands into Bully, who rush to shoot Hands as Hands shoots Gina's hands. Her gun falls as she yells. Rich is in a beaten, weaken, frail spell. Frantic as hell, he rolls under some shelves, quicker than brass shells. Camilla catches one in the leg, two in her back, as she runs. She leaves a little blood trail before she falls and knocks over a roll of duct tape, tools, and nails.

Powell shoots Grands twice. Once in the shoulder and in the stomach. He plunges quick. In deep trouble, he yells, "Fuck it, shit!" He drops the gun quick. As for the cops, Hands is one hit. The other, Bully does 'em quick. Morris tackles Bully. Bully punches quick. Morris catches one, gets his bell rung quick. Hands then takes out Bully. Gunfire is his expungement.

Hands being a cop stuns Rich. Rich thinks to himself, *Son, I slipped.*

Grands, coughing up blood, screams, "Aaaahhh! Hands, you're not a cop, you son of a bitch!"

Powell stands over Grands and confirms, "I guess my goal after all was tangible, sir. I finally got your ass and you're dirty as used sandals, huh. Yeah, you're not an amateur, yet we manage tah exceed our normal parameter to battle yah, handle yah, dismantle yah and cancel yah. As for your organization, you vandal, huh, your scandals are blown out like candles, sir. We did it with wire taps, an undercover, and cameras. Yeah, asshole, your shit is in shambles, huh."

Grands, coughing blood, whispers, "Shoot, you can talk to my lawyer. I'm mute."

Powell, swiftly and hard, kicks Grands in his ass as he lies on the floor. Powell adds, "This time you are fucked, for sure. I knew if I stayed in pursuit, your ass would eventually feel my boot acute, without dispute. By the way, the warrants we obtained were easy to execute. We got the drugs and the loot. Hey, I can't believe you're not saying anything. You really are mute."

Hands grabs his bloody arm. He then walks over to Rich to see if he is calm. Hands sits in a chair close to Rich and comments, "A lot of blood got spilled. Three people got killed. How are you doing? Are you chill?"

Rich looks up at Hands and Powell. "Well, I could use a glass of Henney and a warm towel." Rich picks a bad time to joke. In the midst of dead bodies and gun smoke. Rich looks at Powell. "I feel like an anorexic at lunch time. It was crunch time, and ya'll were the bunch with nines. Consequently, you and my people be making the most sense to me, immensely."

By this time, plenty of officers have the place secured. Gina, tightly handcuffed, yells, "All this shit I've endured! It ain't over, rest assured!"

Powell runs over to Gina, grabs her, then slaps her. Rich, weak and in pain, still manages to engage in some laughter. Powell lashes at her, "Me and my guys have been watching you and your cousin since you came in and got rooms at Days Inn. Me and Officer Wayne, or Hands, practice a lot of restraint then, not to commit a slaying due to the games you and Grands have been playing. This is my terrain and my domain you've been tamed in. No more playing, know what I'm saying? We win."

Gina spits at Powell and states, "You lame, insane men, you are out of your lane again. It ain't over. I'll see you bitches at my arraignment."

She grins.

THE END

ABOUT THE AUTHOR

Clayton Allsgood was born and raised in Baltimore, Maryland. He's been free styling since middle school and became passionate about writing in high school. Clayton currently lives in Baltimore, Maryland.

CPSIA information can be obtained at www.ICGtesting.com
Printed in the USA
LVOW080455260113

317351LV00003B/453/P